Luke Munn
Red Pilled – The Allure of Digital Hate

BiUP General

Luke Munn is a Research Fellow in Digital Cultures & Societies at the University of Queensland. His work on the sociocultural impacts of digital cultures is wide-ranging and combines diverse methods with critical interdisciplinary analysis. He has written four books, published in highly regarded journals such as "Cultural Politics" and "Big Data & Society" and been referenced in popular forums like the *Guardian* and the *Washington Post*.

Luke Munn

Red Pilled – The Allure of Digital Hate

[transcript]

Bibliographic information published by the Deutsche Nationalbibliothek
The Deutsche Nationalbibliothek lists this publication in the Deutsche Nation-albibliografie; detailed bibliographic data are available in the Internet at http://dnb.d-nb.de

First published in 2023 by Bielefeld University Press
An Imprint of transcript Verlag
© Luke Munn

Cover layout: Maria Arndt, Bielefeld

Print-ISBN 978-3-8376-6673-1
PDF-ISBN 978-3-8394-6673-5
https://doi.org/10.14361/9783839466735

I told her that what she said might once have been true, but the internet had changed things. There were underground currents, new modes of propagation. It wasn't even a question of ideas, not straightforwardly, but feelings, atmospheres, yearnings, threats.
—Hari Kunzru

Contents

Acknowledgements

I am often asked how I came to work in this space. In the wake of the Christchurch shooting in 2019, Geert Lovink asked if I would like to comment on the event. Pundits had swiftly provided their takes, and yet these explanations seemed lacking. I was born in Christchurch (Ōtautahi) and felt compelled to say something about this horrific attack and the new formations of digital spaces, online communities, and hostile ideologies that it arose from. My response, "Algorithmic Hate: Brenton Tarrant and the Dark Social Web" was published on the Institute of Network Cultures website and received a considerable amount of interest.

There was something both familiar and novel to this radicalization and attack. Ancient forms of xenophobia and racism were being repackaged into quips, jokes, and memes, repeated endlessly until they formed a kind of constant deluge in these digital spaces. Such spaces were not just "mere" tools but influential worlds. It seemed clear that steady consumption and participation within this media milieu, often for hours every day, would shape the thoughts and values of individuals over time. Media was not entirely deterministic, but neither was it benign. Indeed, part of the power here was precisely technology's ability to apprehend and amplify an individual's desire. Online media provided a personalized route into forms of hatred, racism, and misogyny. Instead of a jolt, there was a smooth, stepwise process that allowed users to acclimate to particular communities and ideologies, normalizing them before continuing on into more extreme terrain. These ideas were developed into

"Alt-right pipeline: Individual journeys to extremism online" in *First Monday* in 2019, which also attained significant traction.

Events since then—the success of the far-right in political life, the rise of attacks and abuse, and the more subtle and systemic proliferation of hate-driven media—have only underscored the urgency of these issues. Thanks then goes to Geert Lovink for his original invitation, to Maik Fielitz and Holger Marcks for their encouragement, to Ruth Barcan at the University of Sydney for inviting me to lecture, to Andre Oboler at the Online Hate Prevention Institute for his staunch support of my work, to Michael Grimshaw at the University of Canterbury for asking me to contribute to his edited collection, and to Fiona Martin for inviting me to the SWARM Symposium. Thanks also to all the students and grad students who contacted me about my work in the last few years. Your interest and enthusiasm was a signal to keep pushing.

Thanks as well to all the feminist, indigenous, anti-racist, and anti-fascist scholars I draw on in these pages. As an academic, I know that scholarly work can feel piecemeal or insignificant at times, detached from the loud debates on the frontpage and the fierce struggles at the front lines. But your hard-won wisdom, published in articles, books, and blogs, helps us to makes sense of our volatile world, to better grasp the forces and relations that shape our moment. Each of your contributions, in its own particular way, advances the broader project of building a world that is more just and livable for all.

Portions of the chapter "Gab's Friendly Hate" were drawn from "Sustainable Hate: How Gab Built a Durable 'Platform for the People'" in the *Canadian Journal of Communication*, published in March 2022 and available online at https://doi.org/10.22230/cjc.2022v47n1a4037.

Sections of the chapter "8chan's Playful Hate" were drawn from "The High/Low Toggle: Alt-Right Code Switching on 8chan" in *Navigationen: Zeitschrift für Medien- und Kulturwissenschaften*, published in July 2019 and available at https://mediarep.org/handle/doc/14754.

Portions of the chapter "Parler's Patriotic Hate" were drawn from "More than a mob: Parler as preparatory media for the U.S. Capitol storming" in *First Monday*, published in March 2021 and available at https://doi.org /10.5210/fm.v26i3.11574.

Sections of the chapter "QAnon's Righteous Hate" were drawn from "Have Faith and Question Everything: Understanding QAnon's Allure" in *Platform: Journal of Media and Communication*, published in November 2022 and available at https://platformjmc.files.wordpress.com/2022/11 /munn_have-faith.pdf.

Finally, thanks to my own family and extended family. Your quiet, steady, ongoing care and kindness is my refuge and foundation, allowing me to venture into these hostile spaces and then retreat intact. Thank you.

Drawn into Hate

The image is pixelated and grotesque, clearly drawn by some random internet user with a mouse. And yet, in an age of polished media, its amateurish quality is strangely captivating. With a couple clicks, it gets downloaded and then imported into some graphics software. The user ponders for a second, then hastily types out a question over the top of the image in the standard-issue meme typeface. On the bottom, he writes the punchline, using triple brackets as a coded signal for Jews. With a drag and drop, the image is posted to half a dozen platforms, one mainstream but most from a growing ecology of "alternative" platforms. He sits back, watching the views and shares rapidly tick upwards.

Blazing down fiber optic cable, the image appears in a teenager's bedroom in Ohio, registering briefly and eliciting a snide grin while scrolling past. It surfaces in a cybercafe in Rio de Janeiro and is quickly posted onto a page for an upcoming political rally. It streams into a living room in Stuttgart and is immediately spliced into a video-in-progress explaining the "real truth" behind recent government mandates. The image has now been downloaded hundreds of thousands of times. But that single image is now a thousand different images adapted for a hundred different contexts, each with a new punchline and a new target. These digital variants will spread, not just geographically but psychologically and emotionally, burrowing into the self and becoming internalized into a growing pool of grievance and resentment. As one poster on a support group said of a far-right theory: "It's a plague of the mind, with the internet as the disease vector."[1]

Hate is being reinvented. Over the last two decades, the radical right have created and appropriated online platforms, repackaging racist, sexist, and xenophobic ideologies into novel sociotechnical forms. This is not just a matter of updating hate for the digital age—of translating racist brochures into pixels or setting up social media for a hate group—but instead a much deeper reconfiguration. Digital hate alters the way that hate is framed and perceived, often skirting around the boundaries of what we consider to be "hate." Digital hate changes the behaviors associated with hate, creating some new practices and updating others. Digital hate reworks the consumption and distribution of hate, setting up new circuits for sharing views and spreading ideologies. And most importantly, digital hate ramps up the allure of hate, softening its approach, broadening its appeal to a wider demographic, and intensifying its hold on the self.

This allure helps us to understand the success of digital hate, its rise and rise in the present. New forms of hate are not just novel but successful, spreading more effectively to new audiences and exerting a more insidious influence. Over the last few years, social and cultural scholars have observed this surprising accomplishment. The far-right has become the "near-right."[2] Extremist ideologies have moved from "the edge to the middle."[3] Platforms have sprung up, structuring communities and intensifying antagonisms. Viewpoints that were formerly inappropriate to mention in the public domain are now openly espoused and embraced. In short, we've witnessed a "mainstreaming of hate."[4] Mainstream hate overflows conventional categories like terror and established labels like national security. This is not a niche issue for an elite cadre of government groups and policy experts, but a broad and growing problem that impacts societies around the world. Digitally-driven hate is everyday hate, and it affects us all.

And yet if digital hate is important, its very novelty and fluidity has made it difficult to grasp. Political science has tended to frame the radical right as an extension of traditional party politics, ignoring the novel transformative potentials of the internet.[5] Computer science has excelled at collecting and classifying hateful comments or carrying out granular linguistic analysis,[6] but often fail to grapple with the larger social, political, and psychological questions of how hate operates and why it is so effective. One concrete result of this lack of deeper understanding is that agencies continue to adopt conventional definitions and reactionary responses. Hate is bad, so get rid of it. One anti-hate campaign, for instance, trains youth to identify and report instances of hate speech online so that it can be removed.[7] Yet what qualifies as hate, what gets missed, and what fuels its rise in the present? These projects aim to eradicate hate, yet never fully engage with the online spaces and user cultures that render it logical and appealing.

This book explores digital hate, seeking to understand the potent connection between online spaces and its renewed allure. To pursue this question, I dig into four objects, showing how digital systems and environments rework familiar forces into new hate forms. 8chan is an image board site founded in 2013. As the self-proclaimed cesspool of the internet, it is ground zero for a toxic mélange of hate with violent real-world consequences. In a perverse way, however, it produces *playful hate*, emerging out of a nihilistic space of meaninglessness and memes. Parler is "the world's town square," a platform with deep pockets that aims to provide a nexus for conservative views and activity. The platform became hypervisible as its role in the storming of the United States Capitol emerged. What we see here is *patriotic hate*, embedded in myths of white nationalism yet reconfigured in an era of microblogging and live streaming. QAnon is a far-right conspiracy theory that has surged in popularity by harnessing digital platforms and social media. I explore a year of posts written by Q, the anonymous figure at the heart of QAnon. Q constructs a kind of *righteous hate* by blending powerful religious narratives with modern ideals of skepticism and participatory media practices. And finally, I look at Gab, a newer "platform for the people." Despite technical and political pressure, Gab has enjoyed significant success and seeks to build a sustainable infrastructure and a parallel society online. With its tech-forward products and accessible features, Gab exemplifies a more moderate but equally dangerous phenomenon, a form of *friendly hate*.

Reinventing hate is about enhancing its appeal and improving its spread, rather than creating something new from whole cloth. Already in the descriptions above, we can see the ways that digital platforms are consciously building on a long lineage of hate-based ideologies, from anti-semitism to misogynistic fascism and anti-immigration.[8] These are old or even ancient antagonisms, antipathies built on skin, gender, and religious difference. And yet it also seems clear that understanding these platforms as a smooth continuation of historic hate,[9] or as a mere online extension of traditional politics[10] fails to adequately address their novelty and specificity. The next two sections examine this tension, using the shorthand terms of *the heart* and *the network* to address this interplay.

The Heart

Hate is at the heart of who we are. In their book *Friction*, Clark McCauley and Sophia Moskalenko begin by listing popular stereotypes of radicals: they are evil, they are crazy, they are not like us. One by one, they knock these caricatures down, using real-world examples to do so. For the authors, the first step to understanding radicalization is simple but fundamental: we must "leave behind the orderly and comfortable world in which normal people do not do terrible things."[11] There is a disturbing truth here, a reality that is uncomfortable and confronting. But until we accept this fact and venture into this territory, no progress can be made.

John Horgan makes a similar point in his landmark study, *the Psychology of Terrorism*. For Horgan, the quest for a identifiable "terrorist profile" in the wake of 9/11 was enticing but always doomed. Vast amounts of capital and research were poured into this wild goose chase, producing only speculation and confusion. There is no such profile, Horgan suggests, "nor are the routes into… terrorism distinct in a psychological sense from other kinds of social movements."[12] This statement is startling. It suggests that—ideologies notwithstanding—the journey to joining a terror cell *looks like* joining a religious organization or a sports organization. It implies that the inner motor working to draw individuals in might consist of the same social forces.

We have, then, two observations, both from experts with decades of experience. The first: normal people get radicalized. The second: radicalization looks like joining other social movements. Splicing these together helps us understand hate in a new light. The person who becomes hateful and radicalized is not some inherently evil person. They are not a freak or psychopath who was always heading down this path, but instead an everyday individual, "normal" to the extent that anyone can be called "normal." This person did not wake up with a desire to burn the world down or commit a violent act. In other words, they did not suddenly decide to attack or hate another human. Instead, extrapolating from Horgan, what moved them were the same needs and desires that all humans have: to belong to a community, to be loved, to make sense of the world, and to contribute meaningfully to a cause greater than themselves.

Hate is intrinsically human. The point here is not to overly sympathize with radicals, to condone abhorrent viewpoints and brutal acts, but in effect, to go the other way, to erode some of the high minded assumptions associated with humanism, the lies about progress that we tell ourselves. "If only it were all so simple! If only there were evil people somewhere insidiously committing evil deeds, and it were necessary only to separate them from the rest of us and destroy them," famously observed Aleksandr Solzhenitsyn, "but the line dividing good and evil cuts through the heart of every human being."[13] Fear of a world gone amok, bewilderment at a society we no longer recognize, repulsion at people who are different from us—these are all deep-seated emotional responses that can be drawn on by anyone. We can dismiss them, rationalize them, or bury them deep beneath layers of progressive platitudes. And yet as John Gray quips, "the idea of morality is just an ugly superstition."[14] The same subterranean energies are still there, waiting to be taken up by a compelling narrative, directed at a suitable target, and honed into a formidable weapon. Scratch a human and you'll eventually find the hate underneath.

Of course, hate really presents itself so nakedly as hate. Instead, as Sara Ahmed notes, hate does its work of justifying and persuading through another core emotion: love.[15] It is love for our family, love for our race, and love for our country that stirs our hearts. We identify others who share this love and unite with them to uphold and protect it. And we oppose—violently if necessary—those who threaten the objects of our love. Ahmed draws her examples from more conventional fascist and white supremacist organizations, but the same rationale for hate appears in many of the case studies in this book. In the chapters that follow, we'll repeatedly see hate presented in the logic of love: love for the white race, love for vulnerable children, love for the traditional family, love for religious freedom, and love for the nation and its founding principles.

There is nothing new about these objects of love (and hinges for hate). They are longstanding or even ancient drivers of antagonism. They have existed long before our present age and the contemporary information technology associated with it. They are already-existing repositories, drawn from the past. Each is a storehouse of hate, providing a compelling account of the world, a highly articulated set of arguments and grievances, and a rich cast of heroes, victims, and scapegoats. One of the key points here is that digital hate builds from hinges that are already embedded in our sociocultural systems. In a sense, this is the source code that newer code builds atop of. I show this dependency at various moments throughout the book, briefly sketching lines from our present platforms to the racism, sexism, and jingoism of the past. These historicizations stress that our present moment, despite all of its claims to novelty and technological acceleration, does not emerge from nothing, but is continuous with what has come before it. To understand contemporary hate, we need to grasp where it came from and why certain modes of dehumanization (unfortunately) keep returning.

The Network

So hate draws on the heart. This has led some ex-radicals to lay the blame for their indoctrination entirely on their own shoulders, saying: "I did this to myself." In one sense, individuals certainly have agency. They are pursuing something that interests or excites them, they are are making decisions of their own free-will. In that sense, as the previous section explored, hate is intrinsically human, drawing on deep-seated hopes and fears. In fact, this user-centered focus is precisely the argument that technology companies use to defend themselves against criticism. As one product officer said, the user is "the master we serve at the end of the day."[16] They only provide what we've been asking for.

And yet there is also a sense in which these choices are influenced. Groups, algorithms, interfaces, and features all steer behaviors in specific ways. Just as the design of urban space influences the practices within it,[17] the design of platforms, apps, and technical environments shapes our behavior in digital space. This design is not a neutral environment that simply appears, but is instead planned, prototyped, and developed with particular intentions in mind. As Tarleton Gillespie notes, "platforms are designed to invite and shape participation toward particular ends."[18] Online environments are developed over time as a result of certain decisions, and these decisions have influence. Acknowledging this influence allows us to draw "connections between the design (technical, economic, and political) of platforms and the contours of the public discourse they host."[19]

Over the last few years, we have witnessed a confessional moment from the designers of platforms. Designers have admitted that their systems are addictive and exploit negative "triggers."[20] Some have conceded that their sites privilege base impulses rather than considered reflection.[21] Others have spoken about their tools "ripping apart the social fabric of how society works."[22] And these confessions have been echoed with criticism and studies from others. Networked media enables negative messages to be distributed farther and faster.[23] Network affordances enable anger to spread contagiously.[24] These "incentive structures and social cues" amplify the anger of users over time until they "arrive at hate speech."[25] In warning others of these negative social effects, designers have described themselves as canaries in the coal mine.[26]

So if hate draws on the heart, it gets reconfigured by the network. While sources of hate may be racial, spiritual, or epidermal, they are also technical, tied into the networks, systems, and processes surrounding an individual. For this reason, they shift and change as technologies change. While a certain antipathy may be ancient, the *way* in which it is presented and distributed is different today than it was 50 or even 20 years ago. There are new mechanisms and new logics at work. News feeds, algorithmic recommendations, hashtags, online forums, internet memes, digital platforms, and a host of other developments in network media have fundamentally altered how hate is constructed and perpetuated. Hate gets repackaged—and this transformation is not just superficial but fundamental in making it more alluring, more appealing, more likely to be taken up and spread.

As life in all its facets moves online, and ourselves with it, we've become increasingly attuned to the forms of politics and power at this intersection point. Networked media can exert significant force, influencing us in subtle ways. In this sense, I'm interested in how hate is made operational—how technologies contribute to its intensity and efficacy in the life of an individual. This is an inherently sociotechnical relation and I want to hone in on that intersection point between the individual, the digital space, and the community that inhabits it.

Networked media provides a new motor for hate and extremism, as scholars Maik Fielitz and Holger Marcks show in their book *Digital Fascism*. While right-wing extremists may still draw upon elements of classical fascism, their deployment has been updated to the digital age. The role of the party has shifted and the rise of the smartphone has been exploited. Metrics can be used to imply artificial publics and user-created media can be leveraged for panic and fearmongering. For the authors, digital hate is no longer based on formal political parties and far-right organizations, but emerges "organically and strategically in the ecosystems of social media."[27] Each platform has its own culture, its own vernacular, and its own web of influences. This platform-specific combination of elements constructs a unique form of hate, identifying certain enemies, dehumanizing them with specific strategies, and inciting particular kinds of attacks against them.

Indeed, we have already begun witnessing the fallout of platform-amplified hate. Shootings in El Paso, Pittsburgh, and Christchurch have been linked to users on Gab and 8chan.[28] Ethnic violence against Rohingya has been connected to material circulating on Facebook.[29] And anti-Muslim Tweets have been correlated with anti-Muslim hate crime.[30] These overt acts of hate in the "real world" materialize this issue and highlight its significant stakes. This hate is not just a nuisance or a nasty byproduct of online environments but has more fundamental implications for human rights. "Online hate is no less harmful because it is online," stressed a recent U.N. report: "To the contrary, online hate, with the speed and reach of its dissemination, can incite grave offline harm and nearly always aims to silence others."[31] Hate forms a broad spectrum with extremist ideologies at one end. Online environments allow users to migrate smoothly along this spectrum, forming a kind of pipeline for radicalization.[32] In this respect, the hate-based violence of the last few years is not random or anomalous, but a logical result of individuals who have spent years inhabiting hate-filled spaces where racist, sexist, and antisemitic views were normalized.

Of course, we need to be careful to not tip too far in this direction. Contrary to some popular critique, users are not slaves to a technical master or puppets on a string. If digital environments are influential, they are not deterministic. Online groups emerge from existing social structures. Algorithms latch onto existing desires. New platforms cater to existing political divisions. In some ways, digital hate is new and un-precedented; in other ways, it is the oldest thing on earth. This book seeks to balance this understanding, holding platforms and protocols in one hand and emotions and politics in the other.[33] The hate that emerges from bringing these twin forces together is not entirely novel—but nei-ther does it emerge unchanged.

Materials and Methods

We have, then, the heart and the network. The former is shorthand for the individual and their inner-life. Here we are speaking of a person's dreams and desires, of curiosity and "researching for yourself," of their yearning for meaning and purpose, and of their pursuit of belonging and connection to a community. The latter refers to the outer-life of a digital space and its attendant community. Here we are referring to the structure, interfaces, and features of digital platforms, together with the content, media, and imagery circulating on them, and the forms of peer pressure and relations afforded through them.

These two forces are deeply entangled. Digital spaces, for instance, are user generated, expressions of a community in the form of millions of posts, threads, friends, and so on. Yet in giving a specific form to knowledge, they influence how those ideas are circulated and accepted. To put it simply: platforms shape—and are shaped by—people. I aim to probe this reciprocal relation, to examine the interplay between the psychological and cognitive life of the individual and the array of elements (technical, medial, communal, ideological) that feed back into that life. When these forces align—when there is a "symbiosis" between the "inner-drive" and "forms of external reinforcement or cognitive coercion"[34]—the result can be transformative or even explosive. This book attempts to trace what happens to the self when these twin motors are whirring in lockstep with one another.

To explore the heart, I draw on the words of users themselves collected from platform posts, interviews, online ethnographies, and other sources. These are unpacked with insights from psychology, philosophy, political theory, radicalization studies, and other disciplines. To explore the network, I collect and analyze posts from the community, drawing out themes and narratives. I also examine the design and affordances of these platforms, focusing on how they shape communication and behavior. To draw out insights from this material, I turn to disciplines like platform studies, media theory, sociology, history, race, and cultural studies.

This diverse mix of disciplines may seem broad—even too broad. But it seems the allure of digital hate cannot be adequately understood any other way. In fact, some of the limits of knowledge seem tied directly to our siloed approach in research. Computer scientists quantify the precise number of hate posts a platform has, but cannot explain what makes this community and its ideology compelling. Political scientists point to the rise of far-right parties, but cannot parse the networked media that fuels it. Experts in terrorism and radicalization deliver reports about dire national threats, but neglect the more ambient bigotry in our digital spaces and its impact on average citizens. This short list of limits suggests that the tools of one discipline will never be enough. Hate is multivalent and needs a multivalent approach. An interdisciplinary mix of methods and concepts, even if improvised, offers a kind of Swiss Army Knife to pry open hate and examine its logics and mechanisms.

I am interested above all in the logic of hate, how it shifts from being something extreme or ignorant that "other people" engage in, to becoming something that individuals see as natural, rational, or even ethical. Digital technologies are a key part of this process, easing a user into a particular culture and community, distributing and normalizing particular viewpoints, and gradually shunting the self further along this pathway. These are affordances that assist in internalizing hate, in increasing its intensity in the heart and mind of a person, in colonizing the self. By focusing on logic, then, I aim to attend to the dynamics created by specific conditions without getting caught in the weeds. The surge of interest in the radical right has seen too many "explainer" books that list every site, unpack every meme, and chart every minor figure in the movement.[35] And yet such fastidious detail ultimately fails to explain the larger questions concerning the rise of online hate and the allure of these ideas and groups.

This logic is not singular. Hate takes different forms and appeals to different kinds of people. So there will be no grand theory presented in this book. I will not smooth out all the differences and present some kind of universal pathway to radicalization. To be sure, there are overlaps and linkages. Many of the same tropes (crisis, fear, grievance, resentment) will appear again and again. But these are individual and communal stories rather than features of some all-embracing system. There is no singular diagram to explain hate, no generic schema. In fact, hate logics often seem contextual and opportunistic, adapting to a particular sociotechnical milieu. Hate breeds best when it is tightly calibrated to its setting, matching the slang and vernacular of a culture, the practices of a community, and the affordances of a technical infrastructure. For this reason, the book is structured as a typology of hate forms. Each chapter thinks through a form by drawing heavily on a specific platform or community, from Parler's *patriotic hate* to Gab's *friendly hate*.

What is Hate?

But what, after all, is hate? On the face of it, this seems to be a simple question. We have an intuitive understanding of what hate means and what it looks like. But getting past these hand-waving concepts and fuzzy definitions can be surprisingly difficult. Instead of a clear consensus about what hate constitutes, psychologists Edward Royzman and his colleagues show that there has always been dissent and disagreement. Over thirty-three pages, the authors move from Aristotle to Ekman, chronicling the long and contested history of the term. Each era defines hate based on the paradigms surrounding it, from the passions in ancient times to modern studies on hate crimes. And even in the same period, academics and experts differ on what the term means. "In spite of scores of books, topical discussions, stirring editorials, and hate-fighting initiatives," the authors conclude, "there is no single, commonly accepted definition of hate."[36]

One of the problems is that hate manifests in very different ways. In some cases, hate appears to be a violent explosion, an outburst of pent-up rage that erupts in the form of a physical attack. But in other cases, hate appears cooler and more calculating, a simmering resentment or bitterness that drives one person to plot the destruction of another over a long period of time. In some instances, hate explicitly aims to annihilate the hated other, to destroy or remove it. Yet hate may also engender disgust or repulsion, viewing a person or group as unclean and avoiding any kind of physical or cultural contact with them. In all these cases, hate shapeshifts between a range of emotional states, morphing from anger to malice, from rage to repulsion.

How else could we understand hate? To reframe hate, Royzman and his colleagues revisit work from one hundred years ago, resurrecting a study by Alexander Shand.[37] For Shand, hate is not one emotion or another, but instead a disposition tied to an object. That disposition is a kind of anti-love, or in the words of Royzman and his collaborators, "inverse-caring."[38] Inverse-caring takes many forms. For those with significant power, it may be violent and aggressive; for the powerless, it might have to lie in wait and fester as resentment. Yet inverse-caring is even more flexible than this, because it can take great pleasure in the suffering of others, experiencing giddy joy when they "get what they deserve." Here I'm reminded of a disturbing scene of Israelis dancing with delight because they can see the smoke of a burning Palestinian village rising over the wall. Their enemy is in distress—and this produces a spontaneous show of jubilance. Here, hate is not a special emotion, but instead a form of "negative identification" that produces "a tendency to emote in a number of ways to a number of situations involving the object of hatred."[39]

Hate as a disposition of inverse-caring is the working definition used in this book. It is a "good enough" starting point for enquiry and exploration. Ultimately, I'm interested in how online forums, digital platforms, and networked media intersect with hearts and minds to produce new forms of hate. It seems clear that digital hate expands the conceptual terrain of hate, poking and prodding at the boundaries of how we typically conceive it. Is it hateful to watch a video and share it with another person? Is it hateful to joke and meme about race, gender, or religious differences? Is it hateful to create epistemically isolated communities that reflect your values and condemn any others? As the case studies in the next chapters will show, these are not just hypothetical questions, but real-world scenarios. Hate can be ironic and playful or moderate and "reasonable," never rising to the level of physical violence or bigoted vitriol that is often associated with the term.

Not a Terrorist, Not Hate Speech

This broader and more fluid understanding of hate often occurs outside our formal frames. This is unregistered hate, hate prior-to Hate with a capital H. This means, for example, that this book is not about terrorism. Granted, there are certainly acts that fall into that category, violent actions motivated by a political ideology and aimed at instilling fear. These acts are abhorrent and should be condemned. But terrorism also sets up a distinct frame, a limited container. As one government report insisted: "radical individuals may hold hateful or anti-social ideas that many others might find offensive or disturbing. Nevertheless, if their ideas do not extend to using violence or advocating the use of violence, they should not be considered violent extremists."[40] The term brackets out a range of activities that have led up to the point of physical violence, activities that are only ever considered in hindsight, in the wake of a massacre or mass shooting. These everyday practices may be entirely legal and even normal or banal—reading a news feed, watching a video, posting on a forum. Yet these activities also carry a force, shaping the hearts and minds of individuals over time. These small and insignificant activities may stir a person's curiosity, confirm an existing suspicion, or explain a confusing situation. Together, they weave a compelling narrative about who a person is, how the world works, and who is to blame. In that sense, they crystallize a sense of the Other and codify a framework for hate against them. These are powerful forces—yet in terms of the formal and legal definitions of terrorism, they go unregistered.

In fact, this increasingly seems to be a pattern for contemporary violence. In case after case, we see the same refrain repeated: the offender had "no known ties" to hate groups, "no known ties" to terror cells, "no known ties" to militant chapters. Of course, no one is an island: these people connect into extensive social infrastructures and online communities. But they do not belong to an organization or even a cell. Indeed, these young and often unemployed men intentionally withdraw from those around them, embracing their new social isolation as "volcels" (voluntary celibates) or "autistic loners." The Facebook page of the Charlottesville car attacker, for instance, was adorned with jokey images of "weaponized autism."[41] Posts on 8chan champion the same stance, suggesting that "autistic lone wolves (don't) unite. Just shoot more people lmao." This individual radicalizatio—digital and therefore typically more invisible—can be seen repeatedly over the last few years, from Parkland, Florida to London, Ontario. In each case, the offender lacked the telltale signs used to identify terrorists of the past.

As a result, the world is stunned at this violent outburst, shocked by an act that seemed to come out of the blue. But rather than being perpetually dumbfounded, this pattern should prompt us to consider our assumptions. The measures and markers we are currently using are failing. As the far-right becomes the near-right and radical ideologies get mainstreamed, the old definitions of "extremist" or "terrorist" begin to unravel. As one writer noted of an activist who began lashing out with verbal and physical attacks, "the extremist/troll boundary had started to collapse." These are (more or less) normal people who are not yet—and may never be—stamped with the formal label of "terrorist." And yet they can certainly terrorize others. In the last few years, we have seen these attacks take many forms, from doxxing and death threats online to harassment of family members, employees, and politicians in person. While such violence may often be textual or verbal rather than physical, its ability to injure, to frighten into silence, to cause lasting trauma, is tangible. This is especially the case when attacks target those who may already be marginalized: people of color, young women, new immigrants, LGBTQ+ individuals, and so on. Such attacks do damage but may not qualify as such within existing legal frameworks. To address this gap, we need to start reframing key terms and definitions. For Ahmed, for instance, "hate crime does not refer to a discrete set of enactments that stand apart from the uneven effects that hate already has in organizing the surfaces of the world."[42] Such hate lingers just below a legal or conventional threshold, yet its real-world fallout is undeniable.

The same issue applies to hate speech. To be sure, in some of the platforms and communities discussed here, explicit hate speech is fully on display. Racial slurs, terms of sexual humiliation, and other toxic language can easily be identified. But in many spaces, especially newer ones, hate speech is tempered or even invisible. Anti-immigrant sentiment, for instance, can be decoded but it is a matter of reading between the lines. The next generation of right-wing platforms recognize that hate speech can be a vulnerability, leading to legal threats and de-platforming campaigns. But perhaps more profoundly, it can be a turnoff, closing down the community and sabotaging their ability to reach a broad demographic. For its proponents, this more tempered language has huge potential. One content creator "is right wing and edgy—but he also bans racial slurs," explained one user, his audience is "too edgy for Twitter, but don't really want a bunch of slurs thrown in their face" so the Gab group provides a "happy medium." For those seeking to establish a radical right community, hate-without-hate-speech is a compelling solution. For those aiming to increase social cohesion or even just identify and reduce attacks against out-groups, it presents a challenging problem.

At a Glance

For readers who like to jump around or simply want the argument up front, I've provided a brief summary of the chapters below. Chapter 2 opens with the Christchurch shooter and his links to the 8chan forum. 8chan, renowned as the cesspool of the internet, has developed a unique culture over time, its user base relentlessly mocking, shitposting, and memeing in an environment where nothing matters. At some point, however, disillusionment gets tapped out and "ironic" antisemitism and racism poison users, leading them to embrace traditional ideologies like white supremacy. These worldviews are packaged in the internet vernacular of gifs and jokes and shared with a wink and a smile. But their logic of a "Great Replacement," with whites being overwhelmed by immigrant invaders, is a powerful one. This narrative produces an urgent and existential threat that legitimizes and catalyzes violence. To unpack this playful hate and its pathway to violence, I draw on testimonies from terrorists as well as theorists such as Arjun Appadurai, Bulent Diken, and Peter Sloterdijk.

Chapter 3 turns to QAnon, the meta-conspiracy theory that has won over thousands of followers. After a brief explanation of its tenets, I draw on research to highlight uncertainty and empathy as two key factors that prime individuals to embrace such conspiracy theories. I then examine a year of posts from the author at the heart of QAnon: Q. Faith emerges as one key theme in these posts, with the righteous children of light fighting an eschatological battle against the forces of darkness. But alongside faith is skepticism, with Q urging followers to do their own research, use reason, and question everything. These twin themes combine powerful religious references with participatory media practices to produce an alluring narrative and cohesive community. Once an individual embraces

QAnon, it can rapidly transform them, a conversion process that is disturbing for friends and family. Throughout the chapter, I draw on experts on conspiracy theories and belief systems like Janja Lalich and Robert Lifton, together with numerous testimonies from current and ex-followers who describe its allure in their own words.

Chapter 4 explores Parler, a conservative platform with ties to the storming of the Capitol in 2021. I begin by exploring the political conditions that set the stage for the platform, turning first to the election of Trump, who leveraged white nationalism for political gain. In fact, these racialized tenets were always present in the political landscape, and I rewind briefly to show the white nationalism coded into the birth of the nation and formalized over time. This past helps explain the sense of white loss and white rage in the present, two powerful drivers that are emotional rather than rational. And yet if white nationalism orients the subject, its general tenets are broad. I argue that Parler is a key example of operational media, sharpening these principles into particular targets and concrete plans. I show how this media was used in the Capitol Storming to mobilize participants, incite them to violence, and legitimize this violence as ethical or even moral. Here I move from racial theorists like Ta-Nehisi Coates to political theorists like Michael Feola to show how contemporary technologies leverage a link between whiteness and national identity.

And Chapter 5 investigates Gab, the "free speech" social media platform. With its accessible design and tech-forward products, Gab has been a success story for the radical right, adding millions of users to its ranks over time. By creating an alternative ecosystem of apps, news services, and social media, it hopes to create a parallel society that celebrates a set of white Christian values while remaining free of Big Tech "tyranny" and their corrupting influence. Why has Gab flourished where others have failed—how have they made hate sustainable? To answer this question, I analyze Gab News, showing how its mix of topics, sources, and tempered language creates a more expansive, believable, and accessible world. Understanding this strategic use of communication is key for countering it or constructing a more progressive political project. This chapter uses media and communication scholars like Roger Silverstone and Wendy Chun to thicken its insights.

While most of the book explores the logics of digital hate, the final chapter gestures to counter-logics. Rather than claiming to offer silver-bullet solutions to deradicalization, the aims here are more modest, focused on the user and the digital environment. The goal, in essence, is to reverse the mechanisms discussed throughout the book, to pull the individual out and away rather than down and in. To do this, I draw on Thi Nguyen's work on echo chambers and epistemic bubbles, and suggest how to break out of this chamber. While there are technical, rhetorical, and ideological aspects to this process, it is also deeply relational, often coming back to the people that can be talked to and trusted: friends and family.

Notes

1   Schraderopolis2020, "I Used to Think QAnon Was Funny, Then It Became the Largest Cult in World History."
2   Feldman, "Between Alt-Right and Mainstream Conservatism."
3   Wodak, "Vom Rand in die Mitte—„Schamlose Normalisierung"."
4   Wilson, "#whitegenocide, the Alt-Right and Conspiracy Theory."
5   Berezin, *Illiberal Politics in Neoliberal Times*; Mudde, *The Far Right Today*; Wodak, *The Politics of Fear*.
6   Zannettou et al., "What Is Gab?"; Zannettou et al., "A Quantitative Approach to Understanding Online Antisemitism."
7   No Hate, "No Hate Speech Youth Campaign Website."
8   Camus, *Le grand remplacement*; Sartre, *Anti-Semite and Jew*; Theweleit, *Male Fantasies*.
9   Fleming and Mondon, "The Radical Right in Australia."
10   Feffer, "Nationalism Is Global. The Left Is on the Defensive."
11   McCauley and Moskalenko, *Friction*, 24.
12   Horgan, *The Psychology of Terrorism*, 138.
13   Solzhenitsyn, *The Gulag Archipelago*, 242.
14   Gray, *Straw Dogs*, 143.

15   Ahmed, *Cultural Politics of Emotion*, 42.

16   Goel, "Facebook Tinkers With Users' Emotions in News Feed Experiment, Stirring Outcry."

17   Birenboim, "The Influence of Urban Environments on Our Subjective Momentary Experiences"; Jacobs, *The Death and Life of Great American Cities.*

18   Gillespie, "Platforms Intervene."

19   Gillespie, "Platforms Intervene," 2.

20   Lewis, "'Our Minds Can Be Hijacked.'"

21   Bosker, "The Binge Breaker."

22   Vincent, "Former Facebook Exec Says Social Media Is Ripping Apart Society."

23   Vosoughi, Roy, and Aral, "The Spread of True and False News Online."

24   Fan, Xu, and Zhao, "Higher Contagion and Weaker Ties Mean Anger Spreads Faster than Joy in Social Media."

25   Fisher and Taub, "How Everyday Social Media Users Become Real-World Extremists."

26   Mac, "Canary in a Coal Mine."

27   Fielitz and Marcks, "Digital Fascism," 1. See also Fielitz and Marcks, *Digitaler Faschismus*—with a chapter translated by the author to English (unpublished).

28   Mezzofiore and O'Sullivan, "El Paso Shooting Is at Least the Third Atrocity Linked to 8chan This Year."

29   Stevenson, "Facebook Admits It Was Used to Incite Violence in Myanmar."

30   Williams et al., "Hate in the Machine."

31   Kaye, "Governments and Internet Companies Fail to Meet Challenges of Online Hate—UN Expert."

32   Munn, "Alt-Right Pipeline."

33   When it comes to radicalization and hate, agency is key. Quassim Cassam criticises counter-radicalization initiatives for using the term "drawn into," something he sees as too passive. "To describe a person as having been drawn into something is to imply that their involvement is to a significant degree unwitting or reluc-

tant or against their own better judgement... To describe their radicalization in this way is to underestimate the extent to which their political journeys were an expression of their own agency." While Cassam's point is well taken, going the other way—seeing the individual as solely responsible, a kind of atomized subject lifted out of their social, cultural, and technical context—is also problematic. For this reason, I use the phrase "drawn into hate" but stress that it is always a result of twin forces—the individual *and* the community, their predilections *and* the platform, their desires *and* the sociotechnical affordances they tap into. Cassam, *Extremism*, 196, 197.

34   Roger Griffin here is building closely on work from Janja Lalich, an expert in belief systems and cult movements, Griffin, *Terrorist's Creed*, 92.

35   Wendling, *Alt-Right*; Sandifer, *Neoreaction*, Bloom and Moskalenko, *Pastels and Pedophiles*, Hawley, *The Alt-Right*.

36   Royzman, McCauley, and Rozin, "From Plato to Putnam," 3.

37   Shand, *The Foundations of Character*, 1920.

38   Royzman, McCauley, and Rozin, "From Plato to Putnam," 23.

39   Royzman, McCauley, and Rozin, "From Plato to Putnam," 6.

40   Angus, "Radicalisation and Violent Extremism," 2.

41   Fang and Woodhouse, "How White Nationalism Became Normal Online."

42   Ahmed, *Cultural Politics of Emotion*, 56.

8chan's Playful Hate

On March 15, 2019, around 1:40 pm, Brendan Tarrant flicked on the Go-Pro headset attached to his tactical helmet and started live streaming its video. The first-person view, with a weapon at the base of the frame, is eerily reminiscent of the classic shooter video game aesthetic. Tarrant cued up a couple military songs on a portable speaker, and then walked into the Al-Noor Mosque in Christchurch, New Zealand, where 190 people were gathered for Friday prayers. A worshipper greeted this new arrival with a "hello, brother." Tarrant responded by firing at him multiple times with a semiautomatic shotgun, killing him.

Tarrant then dropped the shotgun and switched to an AR-15 assault rifle. All over the gun, words or tags were written. On the barrel: "Turkofagos," a term used by Greeks during the war for independence. On the magazine: "here's your migration compact," a reference to an intergovernmental agreement on migrants. And on the scope: "14 words," a reference to the infamous command of white supremacist David Lane: "We must secure the existence of our people and a future for white children."

Tarrant moved into the prayer hall, where he opened fire on worshippers at close range, killing dozens. He went outside to his car, retrieving another weapon, and killing several more worshippers in the carpark. Once more he walked into the prayer hall, firing on people who were already wounded. Worshippers who were crying out for help were systematically shot in the head. A strobe light attached to his helmet helped disorient and confuse his victims. Finally, he left, shooting and killing a woman outside on his way out.

Tarrant jumped into his car and drove eastward at high speed, veering into oncoming traffic and over a grass median. A few minutes later, he reached the Linwood Islamic Centre, where around 100 people were gathered. At first, Tarrant couldn't find the front door and chose instead to shoot four people outside and through a window. One brave worshipper, Abdul Aziz Wahabzada, ran outside and took cover behind some cars, attempting to distract the shooter. However, Tarrant could not be deterred, located the door, and entered the Centre, shooting and killing three more people.

Tarrant drove away in his Subaru Outback, intending to drive to another mosque in Ashburton, nearly ninety kilometers away. Yet just two minutes later, a police unit spotted the vehicle and initiated a pursuit. Video shows the silver SUV being rammed onto the side of the road by the police vehicle, a rear wheel still spinning in the air. Two officers descend on the car with guns drawn. Moments later, they drag Tarrant out of the vehicle and onto the concrete footpath. From there he was taken into custody.[1]

All in all, Tarrant murdered 51 people ranging from 3 to 77 years old and wounded another 40 with gunshot injuries. These were people with a name and a story, software engineers and students, welders and physicians, accountants and Imams. Some were born in Pakistan and India, others in Fiji and New Zealand. Some still suffer from pain due to fragments of bullets in their bodies. Others lost the use of a limb or will be bound to a wheelchair for life. Child survivors carry long term trauma, showing behavioral changes and becoming scared at loud noises. Other children keep asking for their father and can't understand why he is not there.

While it is necessary to honor the victims and condemn the violence, it is equally vital to understand the logic of this attack. In the perverse logic of the shooter and his audience, the shooting was a kind of violent meme: necessary white supremacy marked up with metadata and packaged as a playful or even viral phenomenon. "Well lads, it's time to stop shitposting and time to make a real life effort post," Tarrant had posted on 8chan shortly before the attack. A manifesto written in the easily digestible format of the FAQ (Frequently Asked Questions) had been posted to 8chan and other media outlets on the same day. And the real-time footage of his spree had been live-streamed on Facebook. Taken together, this exploitation of internet references and distribution mechanisms dehumanizes the victims of the attack and its horrific impact, but also provides a window into a particular form of hate. Indeed, this callous logic feels carefully calibrated for 8chan and its community, where the attack found immediate approval. As the body count rose, Tarrant quickly became a hero who had achieved a "new high score," surpassing the former record holder Seung-Hui Cho of Virginia Tech. Tarrant attained instant cult status in the community. No longer would he be merely an Anonymous user or even referred to with his given name: now he was Saint Tarrant.

Shit Posts for a Shit Life

From the beginning, the "chans" were a playful but ultimately nihilistic online space. These spaces emerged from earlier communities on IRC channels like Raspberry Heaven, where a culture of adolescent mockery had developed over a decade. These channels had originally been setup for fans of manga and anime to celebrate their idols and enthusiastically discuss the latest events in the series. However, as Dale Beran notes in his exhaustive ethnography of 4chan and 8chan, clusters of teen boys descended on these channels and quickly chased away the few women who remained.[2] Anime was not celebrated so much as coopted as a medium for in-jokes, ridicule, and sexual fantasy. Fandom was replaced by derision.

While these communities migrated and expanded, first from 2channel to 4chan around 2003, and then later to copycats like 8chan, this culture of nihilism persisted. On the chans, nothing was sacred. Everything could be held up for ridicule, poked and stretched until it becomes a caricature. In this environment, any earnest statement was quickly ripped apart; any serious gesture was mercilessly mocked. Instead, channers cultivated the art of "shitposting," churning out a steady stream of content that was intentionally low-quality or off-topic. The aim was not to engage in measured debate, but to derail a thread as fast as possible, a task that could often be done by lashing out against other members. Once these flame wars had begun, users competed against each other to create the funniest or most denigrating insult.

None of this content mattered. In fact, one of the "innovations" of 4chan and 8chan over their predecessors was that the structure of the platform itself mirrored this belief. By default, forum software came with a set of features designed to structure content in meaningful ways. Every post had a title so you could identify what its topic was. Every author had a username so that they could be recognized, building up reputation and trust. Every post was stored in an archive for all time, so that it could be easily retrieved and reread. The chans threw away all of these features. Posts were now just assigned a number. Users were all named Anonymous by default. And instead of keeping posts, the platform deleted them in a matter of days or even hours. "All posts were regarded as garbage" on the predecessor platforms that spawned 4chan, notes Beran, "but 4chan actually treated them like garbage."[3]

These spaces pulled in the losers of the world. Beran, himself a long-time channer, spent a decade "unemployed or unemployable, drifting from gig to gig in the service economy," a model of the "idle young men" that the site attracted.[4] If these users had a job, it was generally precarious, exploitative, or underpaid. Many had given up on finding a rewarding job or at least the broader dream of a serious, upwardly-mobile career. Drawing from policy wonk terminology, channers described themselves as living the "NEET" life: Not in Education, Employment, or Training.

The social life of many of these individuals was minimal or non-existent. Beran describes a number of long-term users who rarely left the house. As a result, their number of real-world friends often veered close to zero, and their romantic life had flatlined a long time ago. Some were completely shunned by the opposite sex, leading them to adopt the label "incels" or involuntary celibates. Indeed, a number openly admitted they were virgins or "wizards" and set up subforums dedicated to others like them who had given up hope of ever attracting a girlfriend.

For the self-proclaimed losers in these spaces, life had proven to be profoundly disappointing. There was nothing to look forward to and certainly nothing to believe in. And yet, somehow, life continued. The result, as Deleuze so aptly described, was a "depreciated life which now continues in a world without values, stripped of meaning and purpose, sliding over further towards its nothingness."[5] A depreciated life meant trolling well-meaning people for the lols, it meant marathon gaming sessions and porn watching, and it meant hanging out with other failures like themselves on the chans.

Swamped by Memes, Poisoned by Irony

If nothing was sacred on the chans, anything could be ridiculed. This allows hate to creep in via humor and irony. Presented outright, racism, sexism, and xenophobia are too blunt—or more likely, too earnest—for these digital communities. Instead, they are repackaged in the visual vernacular of the Web: animated GIFs, dumb memes, and clever references. The idea tumbler of the Internet provides the perfect environment for image or language play, for absurd juxtapositions and insider jokes. Impish and jocular, such practices trivialize and thus normalize racism and xenophobia. As one study asked: "can it be hate if it is fun?"[6]

Memes, often under the guise of "edgy" humor, thus form a key medium for normalization. Radical right memes leverage technical functionality to increase their visibility and spread virally.[7] In fact, the chans in many ways cultivated and perfected the art of the meme, constantly finding new ways to mine the limitless troves of the internet, splice imagery together in shocking new ways, and caption it with a playful punchline. Anons quickly cottoned onto the format or template of a meme, applied it to a new target, and "vomited it back up in a half-digested, colorful gush of irreverence."[8]

Such memes are posted, adapted and reposted, being seen again and again. And this incessant repetition produces familiarity in users, a kind of numbness. The first time a racial or misogynistic slur is encountered, it is shocking. The second time, the visceral disgust has been tempered.

The third time, it is abhorrent but expected. And so on. This dynamic is only exacerbated by the volume and velocity of content that digital platforms enable. The sheer amount of posts on the chans and the speed of posting make them less a form of writing and more a kind of deluge or torrent of content that users are immersed within. As Lee Fang and Akio Woodhouse observed, "when users post so many genocide and rape jokes, they become so detached from reality that they become susceptible to the messages of bona fide hate groups, a transformation referred to in forums as 'irony poisoning.'"[9] Shock cannot be sustained.

Because memes are often ridiculous or over the top, reposting them seems harmless. Sharing or even creating new versions becomes a way of reinforcing membership in the community. Yet the ideologies embedded within this content slowly edge their way into the psyche, normalizing fascist beliefs and transforming the individual, albeit at a subliminal level. "I saw ppl negging Jews so I joined in as a meme first off," writes one initiate, "then all of a sudden it stopped being a meme."[10] A few years ago, one popular YouTuber recommended a channel that featured Nazi propaganda behind a thin veneer of humor. When the channel creator was asked if he redpilled others, he responded: "Pretend to joke about it until the punchline really lands."[11]

Packaged as memes, such racist or sexist joking is nevertheless still fraught and must be coupled with irony. Irony provides plausible deniability, a key benefit for radical right initiates within a contested and highly controversial space. Intentions are shrouded online. The distinction between seriousness and satire becomes vague and uncertain. "The unindoctrinated should not be able to tell if we are joking or not" states the writing guide for the *Daily Stormer*, a well-known white supremacist space.[12] This allows racist, sexist, or xenophobic statements to be made, but also enables a hasty retreat when the speaker comes under fire. "Irony has a strategic function," asserts researcher Alice Marwick, "It allows people to disclaim a real commitment to far-right ideas while still espousing them."[13]

As one example of this strategy, take PewDiePie, an incredibly popular YouTuber that Tarrant name dropped just before walking into the Christchurch mosque. With 111 million subscribers, he is both highly influential and no stranger to controversy. This is a man who has hired men to carry a "death to all Jews" sign, has used the n-word in one stream,[14] and has called a female streamer a "crybaby and an idiot" for demanding equal pay.[15] These actions have led to criticism and contracts being terminated. But the streamer is also affable and funny, emanating a carefree attitude, the perfect conduit for ironic racism. That meme was produced tongue-in-cheek. That content was shared to show how ridiculous racists are. Quit being overly sensitive. "Far from a harmless joke," concluded one journalist, "I've come to understand that 'ironic racism' is integral to the alt-right's indoctrination strategy."[16]

Tarrant was well aware of the power of memes. "Create memes, post memes, and spread memes," he ordered, "memes have done more for the ethno-nationalist movement than any manifesto." The Christchurch shooting itself, as mentioned in the introduction, could be understood as a kind of meta-meme, brimming with references to racist heroes, white supremacist phrases, and violent events from history. The weapon itself is literally covered with phrases that essentially function as hashtags. The manifesto is packed with web references and in-jokes. The live-stream starts with the murderer urging viewers to "subscribe to PewDiePie." And even in his courtroom appearance, Tarrant formed a brief "OK" gesture with his fingers, a symbol jokingly "hijacked" by the radical right as a prank on the media and later adopted in earnest by white supremacists and neo-Nazis.

This piling up of references created a densely memetic form, a meta-meme aimed at attaining maximum virality. Unfortunately, this strategy proved highly successful, ensuring that the action achieved heavy exposure on mainstream media and circulated widely. It attained the same success on 4chan and 8chan, with aspects of the meta-meme frequently being shared, from stills of Tarrant celebrating how "based" he is to crude pictures of Clown Pepe holding up Tarrant's gun. There is a powerful kind of feedback loop at work here. Online images circulate on the chans, inspiring real world activity, while real world activity, "marked up" with memes and references, feeds back into internet hate havens, where it is used to canonize mass murderers and their actions.

From Passive to Radical Nihilism

The normalization of hate through memes paves the way for it to be taken up in earnest. Irony sets the stage for more serious indoctrination. After a number of years, Beran began to notice a change in the tone of posts on the chans. "Posters hardly bothered to cloak their anger and sadness in layers of irony anymore," he noted. "Many simply confessed their abject resentment. Promises of murders, suicides, and mass shootings had always bounced around the boards, but often remained unverified or later proved to be hoaxes. Now these threads were becoming incrementally more real."[17]

This change in attitude resonates with the model of nihilism laid out by philosopher Bulent Diken. For Diken, the emptying of spiritual significance that characterizes modern life results in two distinct responses. There is a passive nihilism, a "world without values" marked by a kind of fatalistic acceptance.[18] Here life becomes hollow, reality is "devoid of aim, unity and truth" and everything is reduced to a surface.[19] Subjects achieve some degree of hedonistic pleasure by endlessly repeating meaningless rituals. This is a post-political space, where nothing will ever change. Then there is a radical nihilism that Diken summarizes as "values without a world."[20] Ideologies are embraced with a white knuckle grip, but there is no place for these extreme beliefs or the person who holds them. Subjects often turn to despair or spite, seeking to destroy the world and themselves because they cannot bear its current state.

How does someone move from passive nihilism to radical nihilism? The answer, for Diken, is hate. "Hate is today's radical nihilist 'fatal strategy' against passive nihilism," he writes, "an intense but desperate strategy against the indifference which post-politics brings with it."[21] Hate rouses the passive nihilist from his apathy. It is a "way to introduce passion into the world of passive nihilism, to mobilize the hedonist."[22] If properly cultivated in the mind of the subject over time, it can become an explosive force, generating enough inertia to reach escape velocity, to move him beyond his own downward tug of depression and self-loathing. This energy chimes with Roger Griffin's work on radicalization, where he describes a process "of overcoming a deep experience of humiliation, of exacting revenge through retributive violence, or of transcending a sense of worthlessness and emptiness by finding a specific cause which seems self-evidently important and 'real.'"[23] This might be described as a slow conversion from laissez faire hedonism to steely-eyed fanaticism.

Where do individuals draw their hate from? A single individual has limited resources. They may have had an experience early in their life they can tap into. They may have encountered someone who seems to embody or "prove" the prejudices they hold. But the pool of these radicalizing experiences and encounters, and the antipathy they can produce, is ultimately limited. "The person who hates initially draws on her own rage supply," writes Peter Sloterdijk, "even at the risk of using up her capacity for experiencing rage." Sooner or later the well will run dry.

What is needed is some mechanism for replenishing hate. Rage is too temporary, too ephemeral. It may appear for a moment, and even explode in some brief attack—a racial slur, a toxic comment—but then just as quickly evaporate. Catharsis achieved; antagonism poured out. Instead, this rage must be crystallized into something more solid, poured into something with more staying potential. For Sloterdijk, it is ideology that achieves this transformation. "When rage becomes hatred we can witness the basic operations of ideology formation because conceptual fixations are the best preservative for ephemeral responses."[24] Ideology provides a structure for rage, a scaffolding for fury. Ideology slots this free-floating antipathy into an established framework. This framework works on an immediate level to move rage into a more articulated hate. Ideology "reminds" the subject constantly who the target of hate is, it helps to focus it, to sharpen it to a point, to fix it on a particular object.

If ideology works to focus hate, it also offers a far more expansive pool of ideas and resources to draw upon. Ideologies have been established over years, decades, or centuries, and in this sense they represent the collective effort of many lives. They are collaborative edifices, composed of thoughts and experiences from many times and places. Ideologies, then, historicize hate, providing a grand narrative that often rationalizes the supremacy of one group over another. Rage moves from "a blind form of expenditure in the here and now to a far-sighted, world-historical project of revolution for the sake of those who have been humiliated and offended."[25] The result is a rich bank of hate, a deep well that goes far beyond what an individual can muster up.

High Theory

What ideology do individuals in these digital spaces turn to? There is a distinct set of beliefs and values that circulate on the chans. These are championed and celebrated, whether through overt or sideways praise or simply through reposting and repetition. However, if "ideology" implies something cohesive and overly serious, this is certainly not the case. On 4chan and 8chan, there is a kind of playful ping pong between the intellectual and anti-intellectual, flicking between academic theories and a populist ideology of "anti-theory" built on memes and humor. I call this hybrid blend the "high-low toggle."[26] Groups sustain their ideas by rapidly code switching between the high culture of scientific rationalization and institutional legitimacy and the low culture of populist tropes and crude humor.

These distinct intellectual/anti-intellectual strains can appeal to different kinds of individuals. But they also provide a kind of epistemic switch, providing flexibility to truth claims. When a community is painted as uneducated or naive, pivot to facts, theory, and pseudoscience. When this intellectual and "empirical" material fails to prove your prejudice, then switch to populist rhetoric that proclaims fake news and the elite as sheep. There is no cognitive dissonance here, no jolt. Indeed, reading through dozens of posts on 8chan, it's remarkable just how smooth this slide is from one mode to another.

First, the intellectual strain. Intellectual arguments occur throughout 8chan and resonate with a broader attraction to intellectualism in alt- and radical right communities. Whether or not these arguments are grounded in any empirical, demonstrable evidence is beside the point here. It is the rhetoric of academic language, of scientific proof, of logical analysis, that is key. As Stephanie Hartzell notes, "purposeful construction of an intellectually grounded 'alt -right' provides an air of legitimacy to the ideological assumptions of white superiority."[27] This rhetoric not only rationalizes ideologies, but does so typically through a detached presentation of the "facts" as they are. The all-too-obvious nastiness of former racial tropes is obfuscated, repackaged for a contemporary audience with "a shiny veneer of intellectual sophistication."[28]

Take one "solutions megathread" on 8chan, for example. For this user, solving the racial problems in society will require intelligent foresight and the implementation of a strategic response. The post explains that: "We discuss and brainstorm solutions to the many obvious problems that plague us today. Rather than being simple ('just, like, fix things'), or retarded ('hurr durr gas the kikes race war now'), write as much as fucking possible—outline the specific problem, then detail what exact solution you believe should be put forth. Other anons should point out potential flaws, and we aim to constructively build up each other's ideas in order to create better and more effective designs."

Here the Enlightenment ideals of science and engineering converge in full force. According to the post's author, a problem should be stated and a hypothetical solution introduced using precise language. These are then to be analyzed by peers, with various flaws being corrected and more optimal methods proposed. Although not exactly erudite in its formulation, this vision of cool analysis and empirical investigation corresponds closely to broader radical right terms like racial science. Indeed, one key marker of racial difference in this science is the intellect itself, a pseudo-scientific data point leveraged to justify ideologies. Racial superiority is defined and "proven" by cognitive superiority. In the speech that coined the term alt-right, so-called paleoconservative Professor Emeritus Paul Gottfried posited that "human cognitive disparities" were "stark fact."[29] In its academic language and calls to reason, Gottfried's speech anticipated the exact strain of discourse evidenced in this 8chan post.

Another 8chan post draws upon the theoretical framework of intersectionality. Intersectionality was originally coined by black feminist scholar Kimberlé Williams Crenshaw in 1989 and was aimed at exploring how interlocking systems of power impact marginalized groups.[30] However in this 8chan post, intersectionality is reworked for an altogether different purpose. "The time has come to develop what I call right-wing intersectionality against the Judeo-egalitarian tyranny," the poster asserts. This theoretical model would assist radical right activists in "triggering or exacerbating racial, ethnic, religious, sexual and religious tensions every-where and all the time." The repurposing of theories like intersectionality suggests a movement which understands that intellectual theory can be both valuable and influential. The university is not only the source of such theories, but the very bastion of political correctness, and consequently a key site of cultural contestation.

Interest in wide-ranging and often difficult texts is also evidenced. One 8chan post of recommended reading for ecofascism/deep ecology listed a number of academic and philosophical books such as *The Question Concerning Technology* by Martin Heidegger, *The Impeachment of Man* by Savitri Devi, and *Can Life Prevail?* by Pentti Linkola. Like the theory of intersectionality described above, this literature was conceived for different purposes in another context, but might still be repurposed as a literary weapon for the radical right. Another post dismisses recent books by alt-right blogger Laura Southern as "trash," literary pulp that could distract readers from "giants like Evola," the Italian philosopher and fascist intellectual. Other posts on 8chan mirror this kind of intellectual snobbery. The first response to one post referencing the Masons is not encouragement but rather a critique of their textual sources. "The trouble with Masonic history books is that most are written by Masons, and they're terrible historians," the user opines, going on to recommend a range of superior books. Carefully selected, excerpted, and shared, such texts draw from the past and the present to form an ever-expanding library, providing a theoretical scaffold for the contemporary radical right.

These observations drawn from 8chan resonate with wider insights about the radical right. Groups often display a penchant for literature, extracting nuggets of racist ideology from a wide range of historical, classical, or philosophical texts. Donna Zuckerberg notes that, along with a fascination with classicists like Homer and Marcus Aurelius, alt-right advocates are "particularly interested in the histories of Great

Britain, Germany, and Russia, especially the medieval period, and they also compose and cite articles about evolutionary psychology, philosophy, biology, and economics."[31] In their erudition and their ability to precisely formulate a racial-national vision, such texts form a conceptual corpus that is woven into speeches and strategies. White supremacist icon Richard Spencer, for instance, draws arguments from the writings of philosopher Friedrich Nietzsche as well as those of Nazi-era political theorist Carl Schmitt.[32] Respected or even revered, such texts contribute a historical and moral authority to ideas that would otherwise be dismissed.

Low Trash

However, right alongside this "high" strain of intellectual theories and scientific proofs is a "low" current of populist tropes and crude humor. In this vision, mainstream media is a lie, scientists are biased or bought off, and the government is mired in a swamp of corruption. The general version of reality presented to the public is skewed, manufactured by a liberal elite. In the face of these conditions, nothing can be trusted. The only thing to do is to teach yourself, to rely on your own gut feelings, or in the end, to laugh at the absurdity and play the role of the troll or clown.

This low strain can be found easily when scanning through 8chan. One post asserts self-education over that provided by the ivory tower of the institution: "wrong, shit for brains. You musta got your 'knowledge' from a university. LOL." Implicit here is the idea that the official instruction provided by the university is carefully censored, inferior to the unfiltered knowledge obtained by those who are self-taught. Another poster responded to a news link with a simple dismissal: "no one trusts journos, they're just useful idiots."

Such rhetoric reflects a broader right-wing disillusionment and distrust. Mainstream media cannot be counted on to report the facts fairly. Information from official sources like government bureaus and scientific institutes has been manipulated to suit a certain agenda. These statements reflect a disenchantment with experts and epistemological claims, a pessimism or even sarcasm concerning grand theories. As Nesta Devine notes, these radical right communities occupy a world that is neither modern nor post-modern, a world where "education, science, economics and religion have all failed to deliver on their promised truths."[33] Trust has been thoroughly exhausted, and the result is a deep-seated cynicism.

One way this anti-intellectual strain manifests is through language, a tactical use of words. For instance, one 8chan post highlighted the Terrorist Prevention Act of 2019 that (at that time) had just been released. This long document explicitly called out radical right communities, stressing that: "White supremacists and other far-right-wing extremists are the most significant domestic terrorism threat facing the United States." However, rather than rationalizing their beliefs with theory or drawing on legal arguments to debate the definition of terrorism, the first response from forum members was deliberately swift and stupid: "gaaay… just shoot more people lmao [laughing my ass off]." The language here is aggressive and colloquial, a perfect inversion of the formal proclamations of Congress.

"Gay" in this post joins other racial, sexual and political slurs on 8chan like "fag," "shitskin," "cuck" (from cuckold), and "libtard" (liberal retard). This kind of language does not lay out an array of suppositions. It does not strive to lead the listener through a logical sequence to an unassailable conclusion. Indeed, it is not interested at all in debate or argument, in crafting ideas so that they become the best ideas and win in the public sphere. No, these words are designed to stop the flow of other words, to shut down language. As ad hominem attacks, they seek to terminate any further argument by annihilating the reputation of the speaker. These toxic phrases cut off debate midstream and ensure it quickly descends into digital mudslinging.

Another response to the same post is similarly swift, stupid, and playful. An image of Clown Pepe wearing his typical rainbow wig is slapped underneath, accompanied by his two-word catchphrase: "HONK HONK." While Clown Pepe is certainly racist, the key point here is that he is absurdist, an anti-intellectual, anti-political jester who responds to the ostensible collapse of the Western world the only way possible—with laughter. As Jean-Paul Sartre once said of an older xenophobic generation, they "are amusing themselves, for it is their adversary who is obliged to use words responsibly, since he believes in words. The anti-Semites have the right to play."[34]

On 8chan, play also takes the form of meme generation. Images are cut and spliced together. Illustrations are hastily redrawn. The results are uploaded to the board, throwing them back out to the community, where they can be remade once more. The aim of all this visual production is to land—partially by careful refinement, partially by chance and crowd-sourcing—on the next viral phenomenon. Memes win through repetition, not argumentation. Their end game is not to construct a logical argument, but rather to saturate an environment like a message board or even the wider web. Stamped across 4Chan, Reddit, YouTube, and Facebook—or whatever the platform of the moment is—successful memes follow the user, appearing again and again in different contexts. Such images are not texts, which can be semantically deconstructed to discover meaning, but rather webs of references only understood by insiders. Rather than writing, they should be understood as a performative play that daily reinforces the boundaries of the red pilled community.

"A new breed of populist demagogue has arisen, with no care for facts, reason or data," observed Elif Shafak, "yet alongside this has been a silent shift: the emergence of a radical right wing intelligentsia."[35] Shafak puts her finger on the two strains shown above: the intellectual versus the anti-intellectual. And yet this statement also implies two separate groups or two cleanly divided rhetorical strategies. Peterson versus Trump. "Racial realism" versus racial slurs. What we see instead on 8chan is how entangled these two strains are, with community members flicking back and forth as needed. In fact, there is some proof that radical right members understand the power of this hybrid approach. In a post for the neo-Nazi site, *the Daily Stormer*, editor Andrew Anglin explained that the "headspace of those in the movement" is a place "where irony and vulgarity meet conscious idealism, futurism and a deep reverence for objective, scientific data."[36]

The ability to seamlessly pivot back and forth between high intellectualism and low populism, then, becomes a strength, a way to sustain claims and community. While these two modes may be logically opposed, making different kinds of appeals and claims, they are functionally complementary, propping each other up when one fails to achieve the desired result. Intellectualism engenders a certain legitimacy: academic language provides a dispassionate presentation to racist theories and scientific logic lends them an empirical foundation. Yet as soon as this begins to falter, an individual can shift over to anti-intellectualism, can claim the truth has been censored or covered up, or can simply retreat to the "luls" of memes and mockery.

Mazeway Resynthesis

The high-low toggle suggests a kind of normality or even banality to radicalization, an improvised, everyday quality that can sometimes be missed in other accounts. For example, in his book and article *Modernity and Fascism*, Roger Griffin uses the concept of the mazeway resynthesis to unpack the process of indoctrination.[37] Originally coined by an anthropologist, the mazeway was described as "the total complex of generalizations about the body in which the brain is housed, various other surrounding things, and sometimes even the brain itself."[38] The mazeway gives meaning to messages; it is the scaffolding through which we understand ourselves and the world around us. This mazeway must correspond closely with reality, but for some individuals, there comes a crisis point where it fails to, where the "disillusioned member of a society realizes that the sociocultural system no longer does, or perhaps never did, operate according to the principles which his maze way assigned to it."[39] For Griffin, then, mazeway resynthesis is the process of constructing a new world view that provides order and meaning.

Griffin is an astute and experienced scholar, and mazeway resynthesis is a tool among other tools used to understand this process. Yet some of this work has been criticized for suggesting that radicalization is both more spiritual and more systematic than it really is. Mazeway resynthesis, taken at face value, conjures up an image of an individual who comes to some kind of existential crisis, where her understanding of herself, her culture, and the world around her no longer bears up under scrutiny. She goes to work, systematically deconstructing her former assumptions and clearing out the maze. Ever the rational thinker, she holds up potential new concepts to the light, and piece-by-piece, slowly introduces them to her mazeway, establishing once again the tidy hedgerows and neat pathways. The mazeway resynthesis is complete.

The real world, of course, looks nothing like this. While some ex-radicals do speak of a kind of spiritual or existential crisis, others talk more humbly about feeling isolated and alone, about finding meaning and comfort, or simply about being bored and deeply depressed. These individuals are not saints who have lost some transcendent spark, but rather ordinary people who begin to feel that their once-held-assumptions no longer hold up. To be sure, they do go searching for something else, for something more, but they are not a "brain in a box" and that search does not take place alone. Firstly, it occurs in a social context, where others are able to offer empathy and encouragement. For many radicals, it is less about embracing ideas and more about embracing a community, which provides membership and meaning. And secondly, this occurs in a networked context, where internet technologies can latch onto behavior and shape it in significant ways. Search queries are autocompleted, engagement algorithms are deployed, related videos are recommended. In this sense, mazeway resynthesis is not something that emerges purely from the drive of the individual, but also in concert with the dialogue of community members and the responsiveness of computational features. Desire is augmented (and even anticipated) at every step by social and technical systems.

How does this resynthesis take place? Not systematically, through a rigorous review of competing ideologies, until one is chosen and taken, fully formed, off the shelf, but rather through a much more organic process. Flicking through a social media feed, or a forum thread, or a video playlist, individuals come across an image or idea that resonates with them. The user identifies with a certain value or claim that reworks what they had once assumed and forms one strut in a new framework. This is not to suggest a completely random process of indoctrination; there are clearly overlaps both ideologically and organizationally between white supremacy and religious fundamentalism, for instance, or between fascism and antisemitism. But these capital "I" ideologies are abstractions that the individual cannibalizes for his actual worldview, which is a far more mixed affair. This mongrel construction may feature an element of Aryan paganism but also include fragments of conservative Christianity; it could revolve around hyper masculinity and misogyny, yet also solder in some tenets of anticapitalist critiques. The result is a kind of "scavenger ideology."[40]

Of course, ideological formation has long worked in this piecemeal fashion. An individual in the past may have cobbled together ideas from childhood stories with more recent racial encounters and pet phrases lifted from a hate group tract. Yet the internet vastly amplifies the ability of individuals to construct a highly articulated worldview from an enormous array of sources. For one, there is the incredible depth of information online. Every topic can be researched and investigated. Every obscure and esoteric text is now available. Every microfandom and niche movement has its own community. For another, this networked space is inherently nonlinear, built on the paradigm of the hyperlink and interconnected servers. This allows users to flick from link to link and platform to platform, springing from one set of ideas to another in a matter of seconds. As the individual browses, they discover conceptual links between worldviews, taking shards of these disparate intellectual (or anti-intellectual) traditions and soldering them into their own new ideological formations.

Tradition and the Zero-Sum Game

So when we look at spaces like "/pol" on both 4chan and 8chan, we see a mélange of fascism, hyperconservatism, white supremacy, and other radical right ideologies. In fact, "/pol" was originally created as a kind of isolation chamber, a way to shift neo-Nazis into a bracketed off section of the site away from the main news section. And in one sense, the strategy worked: these users and the ideology they touted did migrate across to this new space. But as Beran notes, "the board didn't get crowded out in the marketplace of ideas. Rather, 4chan's new neo-Nazi section thrived."[41]

On an immediate level, the popularity of these ideologies can be chalked up to fit. These worldviews elevate the demographic that the chans attract: straight white males. Yet more subtly, all these ideologies share a strong bedrock of tradition. For those who have believed in nothing for so long, tradition seems to offer a sure foundation, an ideological rock to latch on to. "To isolated people adrift in nihilistic determinism" writes Beran, "the easy fix of tradition was a lifeline."[42] There is a certitude to traditional conservatism, a firm moral conviction that its way—and no other—provides the path to a prosperous and flourishing society. In fact, this stability is not just alluring for channers, but for a far broader segment of society who feel that life is unstable and all-too-precarious. As theorist Franco Berardi notes, contemporary uncertainty triggers the rise of the "identitarian shelter," the "return of concepts such as the homeland, religion and family as aggressive forms of reassurance and self-confirmation."[43]

Traditional values are reassuringly straightforward. Indeed, when set against the nebulous world of tolerance and diversity espoused by progressive ideologies, this conservatism seems cut-and-dried. Its principles offer a ruleset that can be followed, a formula that promises dignity and respect if properly adhered to. Indeed, for those who spend hours in a digital world every day, conservatism could be viewed as a kind of algorithm for restoring their status in the world. IF society reverted to traditional roles, traditional religion, and traditional race and gender relations THEN the world would be made right and these young men would be elevated to their proper station.

For the typical young white male on one of the chans, the loss of tradition provides a cogent explanation for his low status and bleak future. Once upon a time, the story goes, the Aryan race was a proud and prosperous people. Society was centered around the family, and the man was the figurehead of this group. As the primary breadwinner, the man could expect to attain a stable, well-paying job. He could choose a committed mate from a broad pool of white women, who would cheerily carry out her wifely duties of homemaking and reproducing. And he could expect to receive several children from this arrangement, who would inherit the wealth and status that he had acquired over a lifetime. This family unit would live with dignity, exercising regularly, attending church, and socializing harmoniously with people who looked and thought just like them. While this tale and its portrait of white dignity in the rose-tinted past may seem simplistic, it nevertheless possesses a strong pull, and there are countless memes floating around "/pol" that yearn nostalgically for these halcyon days.

According to this fable, this idyllic image has been eroded over time by the Other. In a world of finite resources, the rise of other groups (immigrants, Muslims, Jews, queers, progressives, and so on) inherently brought with it a decline in the wealth and status of the white male conservative group that channers identify with. A better life for "them" means a worse existence for "us." In this framing, the prosperity enjoyed by one group is deeply dependent on ensuring others do not attain it.

To understand this relation, we can turn to Arjun Appadurai's concept of "parasitic identities." For Appadurai, parasitic identities are "identities whose social construction and mobilization require the extinction of other, proximate social categories, defined as threats to the very existence of some group, defined as a we."[44] Parasitic identities are composed of two or more identity groups, with one seeing the other as an existential threat. One of these identities has enjoyed majoritarian status and the power and privilege that comes with it, but this seems to now be in jeopardy. Their twinned other is on the rise, progressively gaining in numbers and influence. If the parasitic identity fails to take this threat seriously and to act in a decisive way, then their current "supremacy" could be at risk.

For those who embrace the parasitic identity, the world is a zero-sum game. The image that springs to mind is of two individuals handcuffed together in a room; a bowl of food is placed between them; no rules are given. Here, more for one is clearly less for another. And so the parasitic identity deeply connects the fate of its groups, locking them together in an existential struggle. Already, here, we can see the way in which the threat posed by "them" works to bolster the identity of "us." The darker and thicker this threat can be painted, the more solid those who combat it become. As the image of the enemy looms increasingly large, the identity of the protagonist coalesces, becoming a sharper and more cohesive set of markers related to whiteness and masculinity.

The Great Replacement

Appadurai notes that groups often quantify this risk by drawing on "pseudo-demographic arguments about rising birthrates"[45] among their targeted enemies, and this is precisely what we see when we turn to Tarrant. In his manifesto, population statistics serve as an undeniable argument, providing the hard empirical proof of an existential threat. In fact, he references them three times to underscore their importance: "it's the birthrates, it's the birthrates, it's the birthrates." Tarrant's mantra demonstrates the dangerous blend of elements that demographic arguments provide. Population statistics are quantitative and seemingly impartial, providing an impression of objectivity and scientific rigor. But these stats are spliced and skewed, used and abused in order to rationalize and advance a racist agenda. Integers are cherry picked to "prove" what an individual already knew: inferior others are rising up around them. The purity and status of "their ancestors" must be defended.

Tarrant's manifesto is titled *The Great Replacement*, an allusion to the 2011 screed of the same name by Renaud Camus. Immigration is a "misnomer," writes Camus in typically inflammatory style, "it is more akin to an invasion, a migratory tsunami, a submerging wave of ethnic substitution."[46] Camus' phrase retains the dire threat of former slogans like "white genocide" but repackages it into something more contemporary, more flexible and palatable. The fear of replacement, of a homogenous group with their distinctive culture being diluted to the point of extinction, can theoretically be taken up by anyone—and it has done exactly that. Lauren Southern, a radical right figurehead, created a video of the same name, while mainstream pundits like FOX host Tucker Carlson has integrated "demographic replacement" into his wildly-popular show.[47]

This uptake demonstrates that the Great Replacement is not only adaptable but powerful in its mass appeal.

While the Great Replacement offers white supremacy and xenophobia a friendlier, more publicly-acceptable face, this concept has lost none of its deadly logic. These theories not only urge violence, but insist that it is absolutely necessary. They convince people "that they face a mortal threat, which they can fend off only with violence," notes the Dangerous Speech project; "This is a very powerful rhetorical move since it is the collective analogue of the one ironclad defense to murder: self-defense."[48] These theories effectively carry out a kind of rhetorical flip, a judo-like maneuver that swaps the positions of the combatants. The white aggressor becomes the victim, an everyday hero holding the line against the invaders. The non-white target, passively going about their life, is made into an active soldier, a militant who by their very existence participates in a crusade to overwhelm their racial or cultural enemies. As Steve Martinot explains, this move "justifies the inverse logic by which the aggressiveness of white violence is transformed into a form of self-defense, a self-decriminalization of violence through the criminalization of its victims."[49]

This is why, in many statements from murderers, there is a sense that their actions were unavoidable, that their violence was a forced move. When a bystander asked Dylann Roof why he was shooting those in the church, he replied that he "had to do this... y'all are taking over the world."[50] In his manifesto, Tarrant painted a dire picture of faceless "invaders" swarming into white homelands. Roof and Tarrant have been followed by others who have listed replacement as their rationale for violence, such as El Paso shooter Patrick Crusius. Shortly before walking into a local Walmart and shooting 24 shoppers, Crusius posted his manifesto on 8chan. In the text, he asserts that the "Great Replacement" was his central motivation; the immigration of Hispanics into the country posed "a threat to American racial and cultural identity."[51] In this perverse logic, violence is unavoidable or even inevitable: every attack is a pre-emptive defense.

The Great Replacement theory slots neatly into the zero-sum game world posited by conservative ideologies. In this worldview, nothing can be taken for granted. There are finite resources, and if your group is not actively maintaining its stature and guarding its assets, others will quickly gobble them up. As Appadurai noted, for parasitic identities, there is always the deep-seated anxiety that the two groups will switch sides. The majority will become the minority. Those who used to dominate will be dominated. Given this logic, there can be no sense of stasis, no moment to rest on your laurels. Every day of inactivity represents a setback for one side and an advance for the other. "Time is of the essence," wrote Norwegian mass-murderer Anders Breivik in his manifesto, "we have only a few decades to consolidate a sufficient level of resistance before our major cities are completely demographically overwhelmed by Muslims."

Perhaps this is why the zero-sum game seems to have a unique power to stir men into action. Latent hate, developed over time on platforms like 4chan and 8chan, is suddenly converted into a concrete plan and a violent act. Seething animosity is transformed into activity. "[White nationalists] claim they will defend what is theirs, yet everything is being stolen from them in front of their eyes and they know it," stated Dylann Roof in his jailhouse journal, "they stand idle with their tails between their legs." "Well lads, it's time to stop shitposting and time to make a real life effort post" posted Brendan Tarrant shortly before carrying out his abominable act of violence on two Christchurch mosques. "Screw your optics, I'm going in" posted Robert Bowers just before walking into a Pittsburgh synagogue and opening fire. In all these cases, there is a sense in which a breaking point has been reached, a threshold has been crossed. Thinking and speaking is no longer enough to stem the slow decline of "us" and the rising tide of "them." Something must be done.

The Great Replacement, then, has a kind of easily digestible logic and yet manages to present a life-or-death threat. Its power lies precisely in this combination of simplicity and urgency. And these deadly ideals, lying at the end of the radicalization pathway, highlight the danger of 8chan's playful hate. Memeing, trolling, and shitposting is what you do in an environment where nothing matters. But eventually, this playful emptiness dries up. Racism and genocide move from ironic joke to subliminal influence. In this swamp of nihilism, traditional ideologies offer a firm ground, something to cling to. White supremacy, ethnonationalism, fascism, and other belief systems provide a concrete explanation for a (white) individual's broken life. How sincerely these beliefs are held is impossible to know. After all, these are channers. Perhaps such beliefs are just one more hoax, another bad faith argument that deceives even the individual himself. They convince the shooter that they are a warrior, attaining glory by sacrificing himself for a greater cause. In reality, he is a mass murderer, putting a bullet into a defenseless victim as a way to beat another user's high score.

Notes

1   Tso and Owen, "Video Captures Act of Bravery as Police Arrest Christchurch Shooting Suspect."

2   Beran, *It Came from Something Awful*, 76.

3   Beran, 80.

4   Beran, 19.

5   Deleuze, *Nietzsche and Philosophy*, 148.

6   Schwarzenegger and Wagner, "Can it be hate if it is fun?"

7   Marwick and Lewis, "Media Manipulation and Disinformation Online."

8   Beran, *It Came from Something Awful*, 90.

9   Fang and Woodhouse, "How White Nationalism Became Normal Online."

10   FucknOathMate, "Message from FucknOathMate in Vibrant Diversity #general."

11   Romano, "YouTube's Most Popular User Amplified Anti-Semitic Rhetoric. Again."

12   Anglin, "Writing Guide."

13   Marwick quoted in Wilson, "Hiding in Plain Sight."

14   Romano, "YouTube's Most Popular User Amplified Anti-Semitic Rhetoric. Again."

15 Stone, "YouTuber PewDiePie Calls Lilly Singh a 'Crybaby' After She Speaks Out About Wage Inequality."

16 Placido, "What I Don't Understand About PewDiePie."

17 Beran, *It Came from Something Awful*, 152.

18 Diken, *Nihilism*, 18.

19 Diken, *Nihilism*, 68.

20 Diken, *Nihilism*, 35.

21 Diken, *Nihilism*, 102.

22 Diken, *Nihilism*, 112.

23 Griffin, *Terrorist's Creed*, 93.

24 Sloterdijk, *Rage and Time*, 147.

25 Sloterdijk, *Rage and Time*, 154.

26 Munn, "The High/Low Toggle."

27 Hartzell, "Alt-White," 23.

28 Shafak, "To Understand the Far Right, Look to Their Bookshelves."

29 Gottfried, "The Decline and Rise of the Alternative Right."

30 Crenshaw, "Demarginalizing the Intersection of Race and Sex."

31 Zuckerberg, "How the Alt-Right Is Weaponizing the Classics."

32 Wood, "His Kampf."

33 Devine, "Beyond Truth and Non-Truth," 161.

34 Sartre, *Anti-Semite and Jew*, 13.

35 Shafak, "To Understand the Far Right, Look to Their Bookshelves."

36 Anglin, "A Normies Guide to the Alt-Right."

37 Griffin, "Modernity, Modernism, and Fascism. A 'Mazeway Resynthesis.'"

38 Wallace, "Mazeway Resynthesis," 631.

39 Wallace, "Mazeway Resynthesis," 634.

40 Solomos and Back, *Racism and Society*, 18.

41 Beran, *It Came from Something Awful*, 161.

42 Beran, *It Came from Something Awful*, 174.

43 Berardi, *Heroes: Mass Murder and Suicide*, 100.

44 Appadurai, *Fear of Small Numbers*, 52.

45 Appadurai, *Fear of Small Numbers*, 53.

46 Camus, *You Will Not Replace Us!* This booklet, written in English, summarizes his much larger book in French: *Le grand remplacement*.

47   Penny, "The Deadly Myth of the Great Replacement."
48   Dangerous Speech Project, "FAQ."
49   Martinot, *The Machinery of Whiteness*, 157.
50   Cobb, "Inside the Trial of Dylann Roof."
51   Penny, "The Deadly Myth of the Great Replacement."

QAnon's Righteous Hate

By the time Cecilia Fulbright stepped onto her driveway in Waco at 9am, the sun was already well up, the heat causing ripples and mirages over the surface of the asphalt. According to a later police affidavit, when she unlocked her red Pontiac Firebird and got behind the wheel, she had only one thing on her mind: saving a child from pedophiles. Within fifteen minutes, she had homed in on a stranger's car, a catering truck driven by a woman with her minor daughter in the passenger seat. She gunned the engine and chased them down, but they managed to evade her attacks. Fulbright gave up on the chase and instead turned her attention to another vehicle, a Dodge Caravan driven by a 19-year-old college student. Fulbright hounded the vehicle until they entered a carpark, where she cornered it and rammed it over and over again. By the time officers arrived shortly before 10am, Fulbright had crashed into a concrete pylon next to some gas pumps. According to their report, she was crying hysterically and claimed that the other driver "was a pedophile and kidnapped a girl for human trafficking"; police stated she seemed to be "delusional" and that her blood alcohol level was 0.21%, twice the legal limit in the state.[1]

A friend of Fulbright recalled that she had sent him a message "out of the blue" a few weeks prior with a link to the Trump 2020 campaign app. When he questioned the candidate's competency as a leader, her response was sharp and unexpected: Trump was "literally taking down the cabal and the pedophile ring...one by one," she asserted, "what President has EVEN TALKED ABOUT IT? It's been going on for centuries."[2] Another friend and former roommate had sent Fulbright QAnon material as a laugh, intending it as a shared joke about "how ridiculous" it was. But to her surprise, Fulbright began taking it all very seriously, putting significant time into finding out more about QAnon and its broad universe of conspiracy theories. "I found out later that she was staying up for days reading this stuff," the roommate recalled. "She was getting more and more caught up in it and delusional."[3] In the days leading up to her arrest, Fulbright had gone on a binge of consuming QAnon information. She "had been on a three-day bender on this QAnon stuff," her roommate recounted, "and the last thing she said to me was that the aliens gave her free power."[4]

After first encountering this material, Fulbright underwent a process that fundamentally reshaped herself and her identity. To see this a flip from one political party or affiliation to another is to underestimate the totality of this transformation. Fulbright's reinvention of the self meant a new understanding of the nature of reality, the world, and her purpose within it. Those who were unable to see this reality were ignorant or even evil. Her former roommate recounts how, once she disowned the movement, Fulbright "started sending me these crazy messages attacking me."[5] If she was not with them, she was against them, implicitly condoning the cabal and its plans. "You're involved," the roommate recounted, "I couldn't say or do anything without her accusing me of being a satanist."[6]

What compels a woman to attack strangers with a vehicle? Where do these ideas come from, and how do they move from fragmented notions to deep convictions? To pursue these questions, I focus on the twin forces outlined in the book's introduction: the inner-drive of the individual and the outer-environment of the digital space and its community. In this case, that means examining a year of posts written by Q, tracing a link between ideological content and its psychological hold. Faith and skepticism emerge as two key themes from these texts, a powerful blend of elements that helps explain the allure of QAnon. When it resonates, this conspiracy theory can rapidly transform a subject. For friends and family, this metamorphosis is deeply disturbing, annihilating the person they once knew and leaving a stranger in their place. But first, what is Q? The next section provides a brief primer on the growing conspiracy-theory movement.

In the Beginning

QAnon began on 4chan's "Politically Incorrect" or "/pol" board, a virulent space on a website already considered the cesspool of the internet. A new thread had started in response to a cryptic remark from Trump. "You guys know what this represents?" Trump had asked at a dinner for military leaders, "Maybe it's the calm before the storm."[7] On October 28, 2017, a user who would later identify as Q posted in this "Calm before the Storm" thread. Q claimed to have access to classified information, with the original moniker "Q Clearance Anon" alluding to Q-level security access.[8] QAnon was not the first "anon" on the board to make these claims. Throughout 2016 and 2017, users like FBIAnon, CIAAnon, and WH Insider Anon had all claimed to possess insider information and even conducted "ask me anything" sessions where users could quiz them about classified political events.[9]

What set Q apart from these other supposed insiders? QAnon's emergence from niche community to wider social media milieu was not an organic development, but a conscious campaign carried out by three individuals. Two 4channers—Pamphlet Anon and Baruchthe-Scribe—reached out to Tracey Diaz, a YouTuber who had achieved some success in covering the earlier Pizzagate conspiracy theory.[10] Diaz, known online as TraceyBeanz, posted her first Q Clearance Anon video in November 2017. That video has garnered over 250,000 views and her channel now boasts over 120,000 subscribers and 10 million views.[11] QAnon's spread was aided by a strategic understanding of the internet ecosystem, systematically moving from the niche hate havens to alternative and then mainstream platforms. The trio set up a new group on Reddit called "Calm Before the Storm."[12] Reddit's popularity meant that Q's posts could draw upon a far wider community to develop and distribute these ideas. Over time, posts migrated across to a growing number of QAnon Facebook groups, where the content could be consumed and recirculated by an older and more diverse audience.[13] Eventually this online growth became apparent in the offline world. In 2018, apparel and posters stating "we are Q" and the quintessential Q slogan "where we go one we go all" appeared at a Trump rally in Tampa, triggering a flurry of reactions in mainstream media.[14]

The core fable of QAnon has been laid out by many.[15] In essence, the narrative is that a secret network of actors, from Hillary Clinton to George Soros, the Rothschilds and others, comprise a "deep state" with a nefarious agenda. With its global tendrils in finance, governments, and corporations, this cabal orchestrates heinous acts and hides them by maintaining tight control over the mainstream media. This narrative follows the post-war trend in which conspiracy theories no longer focus on a small secret society but point to a highly dispersed "organization, technology, or system"[16] that openly manipulates a population, if only they had the eyes to see it. Echoing the earlier Pizzagate narratives,[17] Q followers believe that this cabal of powerful politicians, leaders, and celebrities engage in pedophilia and child trafficking. Indeed, the movement has enjoyed a surge of exposure and support thanks to its co-option of the "save the children" slogan and hashtag.[18] Typically associated with humanitarian campaigns, the phrase has enabled Q-inspired content to be widely and often unwittingly endorsed,[19] finding sympathetic new audiences and providing another access point into the Q world.

While these theories spin off in dozens of directions, from blood harvesting to coronavirus as bioweapon, the protagonist at the heart of QAnon is Donald Trump. Whether strategically selected or divinely appointed, Trump is the key figure striving to undo the cabal's corruption before it destroys America and the world. Trump has long been aware of the deep state's dark schemes, deploying his military, legal, and financial power to orchestrate countermoves against them. Through Q's texts and their own research, followers have ripped off their blindfolds and become aware of this reality, beginning a "Great Awakening" that will ultimately sweep the world. While the cabal's monstrous evil currently goes unchecked, the time of judgment is rapidly approaching. The moment of reckoning is at hand, a flood of indictments and arrests that followers call "the Storm." In Q's words, nothing can stop it: it's going to be biblical.

Primed to Fall

Who are these followers and what primes them to embrace QAnon? Why do some people laugh off conspiracy theories, while others seem deeply drawn to them? Here we are talking about a person's traits or history prior to their encounter with a belief system, the pre-existing conditions that make them more or less likely to take it up. This question needs care because there is no "typical" Q follower, no definitive set of personality traits that defines the devotee. In fact, one explanation of QAnon's success is precisely this "big tent" quality, an all-embracing fellowship that manages to draw in climate deniers, white supremacists, hardcore conservatives, and religious fundamentalists, amongst others. The result is a mélange of different backgrounds and beliefs. The Q follower looks like a retired veteran—but also a mother of two, a frat boy with a MAGA hat, and a Baptist pastor. And yet, based on testimonies from followers themselves and decades of conspiracy theory research, there are some common threads that can be identified.

First, there is uncertainty. Belief in conspiracy theories often comes in the wake of a crisis of some kind. Whether on a societal or an individual level, a troubling or threatening event occurs. This event may be existential in nature, destabilizing a person's long held beliefs and assumptions about reality. Or it could be something much more concrete, a shift that knocks out the social and cultural support structures that they have always depended on. For some examples of crisis, we can turn to "How I Fell Down the Rabbit Hole," stories from QAnon followers detailing what led them to the movement.[20] For some, the bombing of the Twin Towers was a critical point. "9/11 was the seed" asserted one follower; I "started questioning the narrative after 9/11," remembers another. For others, Trump's defeat was the event that rocked their world, a "stolen election" that eroded their faith in democracy and forced them to look for alternative answers. "My Q journey started on

11/6/2020," said one, "the Friday after the election." Alongside these well-known crises is the more recent global pandemic. "Losing my job from the scamdemic was the spark," recounted one follower. The "COVID-19 scare," as another follower put it, was a period of major uncertainty around the globe, putting jobs under pressure, personal relationships in jeopardy, and bodily health at risk.

For a number of these followers, uncertainty overlaps with a lack of control. Some crisis has stripped away their sense of agency. In the face of major problems, their existing frameworks—from secular humanism to democratic governance—no longer seem to work. Politics is broken, society is coming apart, and yet the scale and complexity of global issues seems to dwarf the lone citizen. Their news feed bombards them with fear, but accepted paradigms seem to leave them with no meaningful ability to respond. They feel powerless.

These crises shatter a person's sense of stability and security. They set the world spinning, rendering it unstable and even irrational. Nothing seems to make sense anymore. At this point, the subject begins a journey—even if tentative or improvised—of recovering this sense. As behavioral scientist Jan-Willem van Prooijen explains: "the experience of subjective uncertainty stimulates a sense-making process that is aimed at understanding complex societal events, in order to restore a perception of the world as orderly, consistent, and predictable."[21] The world must be righted, its pieces picked up and reassembled. And it is here that conspiracy theories offer a lifeline. They seem to offer more satisfying answers; they trace connections through the chaos; they weave a compelling master-narrative out of our disjointed reality. A number of research studies have shown that this psychological allure is not just anecdotal but empirical. Conspiracy theories flourish in the wake of "uncertainty-eliciting" events,[22] and threats to personal control predict belief in conspiracy theories.[23] In the face of uncertainty, conspiracy beliefs offer certainty and control.

Secondly, there is empathy. Belief in conspiracy can be motivated by a concern for others. Research has indicated that those who connect and sympathize with an "oppressed" group can be prime targets for conspiracy theories. "Conspiracy beliefs actually emerge from social motives,"

argues van Prooijen, "a genuine concern for other people that are victim-
ized, endangered, deceived, or otherwise threatened by impactful and
potentially harmful societal developments."[24]

This dynamic can be clearly seen in the "save the children" campaigns
co-opted by QAnon and Q-adjacent movements. In this tale, the most
vulnerable members of society—young children—are being sexually exploited by celebrities, political leaders, and global elites. The powerless
are being preyed on by the powerful. This story is a horrific and highly
emotive one. It has the capacity to dredge up powerful flows of affect
in those who are moved by it. In fact, in a study of 53 Q followers on
Telegram, "save the children" was the top pillar that drew users to the
movement at 47%, surpassing other core motivators like keeping Trump
in power or COVID "as a control tactic."[25]

Here, once again, we see the way that hate leverages love. Outrage
and indignation and driven by a sense of compassion and justice. This is
why researchers point to empathy as a gateway to conspiracy, especially
when coupled with the other primer of self-uncertainty. Crisis creates a
sense of chaos and uncertainty; in the midst of this mess, conspiracies
pinpoint a clear case of oppression and injustice. But this time, there is
a sense of agency, a chance to speak up and provide a voice to the voice-
less. Conspiracy theories thus offer a cause and a plan, a way forward in
a deeply troubling world.

A Year of Q

What role are followers invited into? What is the grand plan that is presented, the story that proves so compelling? To answer these questions, I
examined one year of posts direct from the source: Q. After all, one of the
directives for Q followers is to concentrate on what he or she is communicating. It is the "messages, information, intel, and facts that Q posts
which are important," stresses an introductory guide, "Anons focus not
on who Q is, but on what Q is saying."[26] Q's "drops" are the foundational
texts of the QAnon movement, the Rosetta stones that spawn countless
discussion threads and inspire hours of online investigation. Here we

are interested in what these cryptic posts actually say, what key themes can be drawn out of them, and how this thematic blend contributes to mobilizing a broad audience.

In terms of method, I adopted a consciously bottom-up approach, allowing the posts themselves to drive the study. Rather than beginning with a grand theory, I focus first and foremost on Q's words, an approach inspired by Klaus Theweleit, whose landmark study "did not originate in theory" but rather in the source documents he investigated. Central to his methodology is that "the material has taken precedence."[27] This approach also resonates with generative criticism in that it begins with the "curious artifact" of the QAnon archive, conducts a "baseline coding" of that artifact by noting key terms and tropes, and only then develops an "explanatory schema" that aims to organize this material in a coherent and insightful way.[28]

I collected a year of Q posts, a large but manageable archive with topics spanning from the presidential election to pandemic protests and corruption investigations. Q often posts several times per day, meaning that the archive comprises a total of 1193 posts. Q posts originally on 8kun and Q followers then meticulously record each drop on "official" archives like http://qanon.pub and other mirrors. Each post appears with a date-stamp, its original URL, and its number. To avoid driving traffic to these conspiracy theories, I reference all posts only by this number.

I coded these posts by reading the post itself and any hyperlinked media, such as screenshots, tweets, or linked video. Coding employed a template-based approach,[29] drawing on my domain expertise in radical right online cultures to define tags but also allowing flexibility to revise these during coding. This baseline coding could be analyzed in any number of ways. However, drawing on generative criticism, I searched for a schema with explanatory power, a way to organize this material that provided an understanding of QAnon's unique rhetorical vision and its persuasive mobilizing force.

I chose to cluster a large number of tropes into two themes that seemed particularly interesting, not least because they appear superficially opposed. The first is *faith*, encompassing tags such as the armor of God, light vs darkness, justice, warfare, and other Christian tropes. The second is *skepticism*, including tags such as logic, thinking, questioning, coincidence, truth, and awakening. These two themes cluster a number of tags, but were also chosen because they are imperatives. Across the corpus of posts, regardless of what the particular topic is, Q frequently commands followers to "have faith" and to "think" and "ask why." These are not just themes, then, but directives issued from a leader to a movement. This discourse aims to legitimize particular kinds of practices and behaviors.[30] These commands steer followers towards a certain way of approaching Q's texts and interpreting the world around them.

"Have Faith"

One powerful command across these posts is the injunction to have faith. Drop #4249 consists of a single image of a lone figure looking across a wheat field, with the words of Mark 11:22 stamped in the center: "have faith in God." Drop #4739 is a prayer that begins with a request to "strengthen my faith, Lord." The prayer asks for forgiveness of sins, for bravery to fight the "spiritual battles in my life" and for wisdom and discernment, before making a swift segue into a cosmic battle. "While evil still roams, the power of Your name and Your blood rises up to defeat and bring us victory against every evil planned against us." "While malicious actions may disturb us," followers will use the "armor of God" in order to stand firm.

As the prayer suggests, a common term within this theme is the "armor of God," a phrase Q uses repeatedly over the course of the year. This scripture passage, Ephesians 6:10-20, is posted in its entirety multiple times throughout this period. These verses, well-known to Christians, enjoin the listener to put on a set of spiritual armor, donning the belt of truth, the breastplate of righteousness, the helmet of salvation, and the sword of the spirit. Adorned in these defenses, the listener may go forth, equipped to do battle with the "powers of this dark world and the spiritual forces of evil."

Similar imagery of battle often reappears when faith, God, or religion is mentioned, constructing a vision of spiritual warfare. Faith here

is less a state of inner unity with God and more a set of outward arma-
ments that protects the wearer and legitimizes their holy crusade. Q's
mention of the armor of God recalls former President Truman, who invoked the same phrase when describing America's battle against com-
munism.[31] In both cases, faith works to expand the territory of the battlefield beyond politics narrowly defined and into everyday life, where it
becomes a more fundamental issue touching on one's beliefs, morality,
and lifestyle. As drop #4545 stresses:

This is not about politics.
This is about preserving our way of life and protecting the generations
that follow.
We are living in Biblical times.
Children of light vs children of darkness.
United against the Invisible Enemy of all humanity.

Yet if this battle is vast in scale, it is nevertheless simple to understand.
On one side are the children of light; on the other are the children of
darkness. This vast cosmic clash takes place between good and evil. Such
clear dualism is characteristic of conspiracy theories, one way the genre
simplifies the messy complexities of the world into a simpler version of
reality. As Michael Barkun notes, these theories often exhibit a "sharp division between the realms of good and evil."[32] This is a Manichean universe, a struggle between the starkly delineated forces of light and dark.

Who is included in these forces of darkness? In the Q messages examined here, there are clear villains that are repeatedly singled out. This
rogues gallery features democrats like Hillary Clinton, Barack Obama,
and Nancy Pelosi alongside convicted sexual offenders and their asso-
ciates such as Harvey Weinstein, Jeffrey Epstein, and Ghislaine Maxwell.
Yet if this rhetorical vision offers well-known figures to scapegoat, there
are also more shadowy forces. A number of drops (#3858, #3905, #4366,
#4385) gestured to Antifa flags and funding, suggested fires and protests
were coordinated by Antifa, and questioned what "organized group(s)"
may be aiding them (#4799). These actors are undefined, their identities
unknown. In Q's rhetoric, these nebulous figures gesture to the limitless

dimensions of evil: there are always more individuals to be identified, more organizations to be rooted out. The labors of the children of light are never complete.

A strong current of millenarianism, anticipating a period of enormous societal upheaval where evil will be dealt with, runs through QAnon. This often blurs into the similarly named millenialism, the more distinctly Judeo-Christian beliefs surrounding the end times. Q's frequent invocation of "it's going to be biblical," combined with the apocalyptic language of evil, punishment, and justice, resonates strongly with Revelation, the Biblical book of prophecy which describes God's return and final judgement, as well as bestsellers like the *Left Behind* series. The conceptual overlaps between conspiracy theory and eschatology are well documented. As one scholar notes, "many popular eschatological texts lean toward right-wing conspiracy theory, particularly in their militaristic patriotism, fears of a one-world government, and virulent anticommunism."[33] For the fundamentalist follower of Q, the vast cosmic battle between the forces of light and dark predicted in eschatological texts is suddenly rendered real and present: the end-times are near. "It's not a theory" stated one Christian QAnon follower, "it's the foretelling of things to come."[34] Faith moves from a dry profession of doctrine to a code through which contemporary events like protests or elections are interpreted in real time. Pastors have admitted that some in their flock have been attracted to the movement, repeating claims of child exploitation and satanic worship as true.[35]

Millenarianism and conspiracy theories both construct a strong sense of friend and enemy. As Wilson notes, the division between "us" and "them" in conspiracy theories parallels the division between the "chosen people" and the "remnant" in millenarianism.[36] The insiders have woken up to the truth and been redeemed; the outsiders have refused this gift and condemned themselves. These themes slot neatly into a broader narrative where the Kingdom of God will be established on earth: the good will be rewarded and evil finally punished. As one Christian political scientist stated, these QAnon themes "resonate with evangelicals, because it feels like part of a narrative we've been invested in for most of our lives."[37]

Across the corpus of Q texts, the injunction to "have faith" derives its meaning from this eschatological framing. Having faith in the end times is a matter of waiting. "One step at a time" reassures Q in drop #4037. "It's only a matter of time" promises Q in drop #3634. Followers are instructed to trust in the broader plan, to have patience even when nothing seems to be happening. Indictments will come, justice will be meted out. Drop #4087, for example, features a tweet that states "be sure of this: the wicked will not go unpunished." Drop #3724 expands on this point, stating:

It must be done right.
It must be done according to the rule of law.
It must carry weight.
It must be proven in the court of law.
There can be no mistakes.
Good things sometimes take time.
Attempts to slow/block the inevitable [Justice] will fail.

Followers must maintain their faith, holding steadfast to their belief in the face of difficulties. And yet, drawing from its eschatological roots, this is not a restful waiting, but a state of hypervigilance. "Prepare for the storm" states post #3880. "Be ready" cautions post #4006. "The enormity of what is coming will SHOCK THE WORLD. Pray." advises post #3728. "Be alert and always keep praying" states another scripture that Q posts frequently. These messages cultivate a mode of anxiousness and expectancy. The world stands on a "precipice" and the next event may swiftly tilt into the "biblical" event of judgement and justice that followers eagerly await. Drop #4732 exemplifies this kind of eschatological anticipation, with one follower replying to Q: "I'm not turning a blind-eye, I'm just waiting for justice to arrive! Let it be soon please!"

The injunction to "have faith" thus contributes strategically to maintaining the QAnon conspiracy theory. On the one hand, followers must practice patience, being unwavering in their belief even when the events foretold by Q fail to occur. On the other hand, having faith means watching and waiting. Followers should be open-eyed and ready, attentive to the small clues that signal the start of the storm, the vibration that will send the whole house of cards tumbling down. Together, these injunctions urge followers to be patient but also nervous and expectant, holding up permanent paranoia as an ideal inner state to be cultivated.

Righteous Warriors

Q's faith-based rhetoric creates a vivid portrait of a vast eschatological battle, a spiritual war of two factions at the end of history. This "hyper-real religion"[38] creates an expansive world and populates it with a rich cast of characters—spirits, heroes, demons, politicians—by splicing together pop culture with Christian fundamentalism, charismatic movements, and longstanding conspiracy theories. Why is this vision so alluring for Q followers?

Ex-QAnoners often point to the emptiness they felt prior to the discovery of the movement. "Is this what my life is?" stated one former follower, "aren't I destined for something more?"[39] In pre-modern societies, spiritual leaders and systems would arise to answer precisely these kinds of questions. In these societies, as Roger Griffin notes, ancient rituals, myths and magic, religions ceremonies and traditions all came together to bring order to the otherwise disordered cosmos.[40] For their adherents, such practices and norms created a distinct zone of meaning within the meaningless universe, a nomos. And yet in contemporary society, this rich web of rituals, traditions, and cosmologies has been pushed into the margins, dismissed as irrelevant or unscientific, or abandoned altogether. For Griffin, these conditions pave the way for "nomic crisis,"[41] where some individuals are confronted by a sense of emptiness, a spiritual vacuum in their lives.

Of course, this doesn't mean that spiritual crisis is the sole driver for turning to QAnon. As one critic of Griffin pointed out, the conditions for nomic crisis are ubiquitous across modern Western contexts, undermining some of its explanatory power.[42] In the face of these conditions, why do some turn to conspiracy theories and others not? Here we can only gesture to the "prerequisites" mentioned in the previous section and an array of other risk factors that may increase the likelihood of embracing QAnon. Unemployment, a history of mental health issues, drug and alcohol use, existing ties with religion or conservative politics, estrangement from family or friends—one or more of these factors are often present when we look at the lives and lifestyles of known Q supporters. Along with these factors, individuals may have had a "significance-damaging" event, where they suffered social or financial loss, and so have a greater desire to rectify this loss by stepping out, committing to a cause, or joining a movement. The role of such a "significance quest" in radicalization has received support from a number of studies.[43]

Soon-to-be Q followers, then, are often searching for significance, for belonging to something greater than themselves. They are hunting for "'cosmic truth' in an ocean of anomy."[44] And here Q delivers. The faith-based rhetoric explored in the previous section paints a stark portrait of a cosmic battle pitched between the forces of good and evil. In this sense, QAnon follows the blueprint laid down by others. In a remarkable passage from his study on millenarian cults nearly seventy years ago, Norman Cohn could almost be describing QAnon: "The megalomaniac view of oneself as the elect, wholly good, abominably persecuted yet assured of ultimate triumph; the attribution of gigantic and demonic powers to the adversary...the obsession with inerrable prophecies."[45] Scholars of radicalization have noted how inductees into radical religious or terrorist groups are frequently presented with a utopia where wrongs have been made right. These stories are "shot through with millenarian or apocalyptic visions of a new dawn or a new era following the collapse of the old society."[46] Like a mirage, this alternative world lies just over the horizon. Ushering in this world becomes all important. Choices have consequences; things matter deeply. This narrative raises the stakes to supernatural levels, and in doing so drags would-be followers out of their mundane lives and its shabby materialism. It is not just any time, it is the end times.

After setting up this grand, spiritual battle, with its two warring factions, Q invites the would-be follower to participate. Who will take up arms against the forces of darkness? It will be you, and you, and you. In doing so, Q's worldview transforms the anonymous internet user into the valiant crusader. "You're special, you're a warrior," was how one former follower said he felt upon joining the Q ranks, "you're fighting the good fight, for all the right reasons."[47] Acolytes are swept up in a grand story that matters deeply. The individual, once floundering in a seemingly meaningless world, is suddenly given a role and a task. Their former failures do not matter. Their day-to-day struggles with work, friends, and family drop away. They are elevated and provided with a new stature. "There was this excitement," one ex-follower stated, "we were joining forces to finally clean house."[48] There is a sense of action, with each keyboard warrior making a meaningful contribution to this crusade.

"Ask Yourself Why"

If faith is one theme, skepticism is another. Q commands followers to question, to think, and to "ask yourself why." These phrases often champion a rational approach. In Drop #4535, Q states that free thought is "a philosophical viewpoint which holds that positions regarding truth should be formed on the basis of logic, reason, and empiricism, rather than authority, tradition, revelation, or dogma." Drop #4494 champions "logical thinking." Drop #4336 speaks of "critical thinking." And Drop #4312 quotes the definition of common sense as "the basic level of practical knowledge and judgment that we all need to help us live in a reasonable and safe way."

Of course, whether conspiracy theorists engage in logical thinking and common sense is questionable. One study suggested that conspiracy believers have a less developed critical thinking ability.[49] Another observed the criticality employed by QAnon followers is always highly selective: sources internal to the community are consumed uncritically, while mainstream media sources are carefully dissected "with the goal of confirming pre-existing perceptions."[50] However, the focus here is on taking these phrases at face value and exploring the rhetorical vision they construct.

Placed together, these phrases champion a particular mode of engagement predicated on reason and logic. Q followers should not simply accept the version of reality that is handed to them. Dominant narratives should be interrogated and deconstructed, a strategy that Q models by identifying individuals, zooming in on license plates, locating financial links, tracking down government documents, and highlighting dubious portions of images. Q is "literally data," said Fulbright, the car rammer discussed in this chapter's introduction, "collected by the white hats and then turned into videos and shit." This work of screenshotting, searching, and document retrieval, carried out in what Q terms the "Digital Battlefield" (#4509), constitutes a contemporary version of critical thinking. For outsiders of course, this thinking is tragically misguided, a form of "apophenia"[51] that mistakenly finds patterns where none exist. Yet for the Q faithful, these practices make sense of the data, establishing complex connections and suggesting surprising new relationships.

QAnon practices, from posting, to researching, and "baking" crumbs into proofs, work to establish new forms of knowledge. But just as importantly, they work to erode established knowledge, rendering it suspect, unstable, even illusory. By creating "closed universes of mutually reinforcing facts and interpretations," what is real for many becomes unreal to the QAnon community.[52] Whether the claim concerns climate change or the coronavirus, the aim of the Q follower is the same: to tear down the edifice of epistemological authority by producing their own digital mountain of contradictory knowledge. Based on a common antipathy towards elite institutions and established knowledge, this work knits together the otherwise scattered pockets of the #QArmy, constituting what Rose See calls a "community of hermeneutic practice."[53] As Procházka and Blommaert observe, such "knowledge activism constitutes the main organizing principle of the QAnon community," securing its "social cohesion in the face of a great internal diversity."[54]

Traceybeanz reiterates this theme of skepticism when explaining her work on Q's posts:

I researched them ON MY OWN. I did not take anyone else's research, and in many of my videos I stated that this was all open source information—it was freely available on the web for anyone to find. And this was the beauty of the Q phenomenon. The Socratic Method of asking questions and pointing people to research for THEMSELVES was an amazing thing to behold. It has awoken more people in a short amount of time than I ever dreamed possible.

Throughout the year, the "Socratic Method" does appear repeatedly, albeit as a decidedly more steered version of the ancient technique. Q will often present a fact or figure and then immediately follow it with a question. Indeed, across this corpus, question marks ("?") occur a remarkable 1700 times. Drop #4672, for example, lists downloads of an item before and after recent protests, then prompts the reader with the query: "Coordinated?" Drop #4673 questions whether there are financial links between Black Lives Matter and the Democratic National Committee ("BLM > DNC?"). In one twist on this method, Q will present two seemingly opposed facts and ask followers to explain them. Drop #4651, for example, concludes with: "Events then. Events today. Reconcile." Rather than serving up the answer discursively, these texts require active work from the reader.

For Q, this is a way to "_ask 'counter' questions to initiate 'thought' vs repeat [echo] of MSDNC propaganda" (#4509). In the Q imaginary, the public has been force-fed lies from the mainstream media. Questions interrupt this diet, providing a starting point for critical thinking and a route to recovery. These questions undermine the established experts and their established narrative. They contest the "epistemic authority"[55] of individuals and organizations who others regard as trustworthy and unbiased. After this doubt is triggered, a void opens up—what then is the real explanation? Q's statements function as "informational cues" to those predisposed to conspiratorial thinking.[56] These statements do not hand the reader an answer, but neither do they leave a response entirely open ended. Instead, Q's prompts typically lead the reader to a "logical" if broad conclusion: that operation was a false flag, this group is secretly funded, that news was fake.

One mode of questioning hinges on probability. Drop #4639 asks the reader to look at "Average number of fires 2018, 2019, 2020" and then follows up with the question: "Outside of standard deviation?" This rhetoric invokes statistical likelihood as an objective criterion for determining the truth and guiding a follower's inquiries. Some events lie within the bell curve of normalcy; others are outliers, unusual, suspicious. One of Q's favorite catchphrases is "coincidence?" Of course, there are no coincidences within the Q universe, nor within the wider constellation of conspiracy theory that preceded it. "Conspiracy implies a world based on intentionality, from which accident and coincidence have been removed" stresses Michael Barkun, "Anything that happens occurs because it has been willed."[57] This is a logical world where things play out in a logical way. Everything has a reason. Effects can be traced back to causes, and if followers cannot always see the gossamer threads that link individuals, institutions, and events, it is because they are not looking hard enough or have been intentionally misled by deep state actors.

Skepticism and rationality is often championed through references to the Enlightenment. In Drop #4408, Q speaks of the movement as a "new reason-based order instituting the Enlightenment ideals of liberty and equality"; followers should adopt these ideals by "undertaking to think for oneself, to employ and rely on one's own intellectual capacities in determining what to believe and how to act." These references to the Age of Reason suggest a new epoch, a revolution that shrugs off the dogma of religion and embraces the rigor of scientific investigation. Now longstanding doctrines can be disputed and experts can be challenged. Everything is open to scrutiny, debate, and debunking. In "What is Enlightenment" Kant urged his readers to "have the courage to use one's own understanding."[58] Across the corpus of posts, Q mirrors this call, urging followers to analyze and uncover for themselves. "Read and discern for yourself" Q urges in drop #3912. "Think for yourself" commands drop #3964. "Research for yourself" asserts drop #4734. "Knowledge is power. Take ownership of yourself" states #4503. "Ask yourself, why?" prods drop #3582. Fed up with the de-facto explanations handed out by others, the enlightened figure dares to take the plunge, diving into the hard truths that lie under the surface of reality.

There is a parallel here to the alt-right motif of being red-pilled, a concept deriving from *The Matrix* in which the protagonist is asked to choose between swallowing one pill and forgetting everything, or swallowing the red pill and seeing how "deep the rabbit hole goes."[59] In the rhetoric of the radical right, this is not a pleasant experience, but it is a necessary one. Within these communities the red pilled figure is the enlightened figure, the individual who has awakened to the manicured reality presented by the powers-that-be and seen things as they really are. In drop #4550, Q states that "You are being presented with the gift of vision. Ability to see [clearly] what they've hid from you for so long [illumination]." From the alt-right to the newer formations of QAnon, then, the concept is remarkably similar: the "sheeple" have their comfortable lies, while "we" know the harsh truths. Propelled by their courage, the Q devotee plunges out of the darkness of ignorance and into the light.

Savvy Skeptics

What effect does this theme of questioning and skepticism have on QAnon followers? How does this new role of the enlightened researcher shape the individual on a psychological level, and how might this reshaping draw them further into the QAnon flock? To understand this allure, we can turn once again to statements from ex-followers. Through articles and interviews, we can gain an insight into what QAnon offered and the kind of pull that these psychosocial benefits exert.

In the myth of Q, Q has Q-level clearance. He or she is an insider, with access to secret or forbidden knowledge. How much exactly Q knows is never specified, but this vagueness is powerful in allowing the imagination of followers to freely roam. Q's drops often given the impression of holding back, of providing "just enough" information for followers to latch onto and speculate about. Q possesses "the truth," whether this concerns collusion between the United States and Russia, the manufacturing of novel coronavirus in a lab, or the sex trafficking of young children. This insider status and the "real knowledge" that comes with it is a gift of hope, an epistemological lifeboat in a time of swirling uncertainty.

For those in the Q flock, this gift of special knowledge makes them exceptional. "Q managed to make us feel special," stated one ex-follower, "we were being given very critical information that basically was going to save all that is good in the world and the United States." The qualities of Q's highly classified knowledge—exclusive, world-changing, enormously important—are conferred on those who read and act upon it. Special knowledge is given to those who are special; to some and not to others. "We felt we were coming from a place of moral superiority," stated one ex-follower, "we were part of a special club."[60] Those inside the club feel they have been elevated, gifted with a new sense of purpose and meaning in their life. Yet along with this new status is a sense of arrogance where others are ignorant or willfully naive. You have a new "level of esteem," stated one ex-follower, but that esteem is based on the fact that "you know what is going on and other people don't."[61] You are chosen; others are not.

One of the byproducts of enlightenment, then, is a sense of resentment. Fury and frustration at those who are unable to see the truth comes tumbling out in the testimonies of ex-followers. "I resented the world, I resented anyone who didn't know what I knew," stated one former QAnoner, "I thought they were blind, I looked down upon them."[62] Here, enlightenment rhetoric and the eschatological rhetoric discussed earlier begin to converge. The QArmy is fighting the good fight. Those outside it, even if they are bystanders, are allowing the sinister schemes of the deep state to go unchecked. Those who are ignorant, who have not "woken up" to the truth, are ultimately lumped in with those who are actively evil.

Resentment works to polarize, to fracture the world into the in-group and the out-group. As Jeremy Engels shows in the *Politics of Resentment*, resentment ends up derailing the demos and any kind of consensus-building approach. While it may be spurred by genuine concerns (economic hardship, lack of political representation, and so on), it is not actually interested in crossing party lines to address these systemic issues. Instead, it seeks to assign blame to others, to carve up the world into the oppressors and the oppressed. Q's posts, like other rhetoric, "does this by orienting the relationship between self and other, us and them, few and many, in such a way that concord is impossible and conflict is necessary."[63] Animosity is deflected away from power structures and towards a variety of groups (immigrants, democrats, "cultural Marxists," progressives, the queer community, and so on) who can be identified and attacked. Finally, there is a scapegoat, a guilty party who can be held responsible for the myriad ills seen in society. In this context, Engels notes, "violence can seem logical, necessary, justifiable, and even righteous."[64] There is a kind of delight in punishing these evil doers, in seeing them suffer. As one QAnoner admitted: "When you paint them as demons, the scum, the most evil people that could ever exist, you don't want to just watch them burn, you will celebrate them burning."[65]

However, enlightenment does not come for free. Secret knowledge, as Janja Lalich noted of other cultic movements, presents both an opportunity and an obligation.[66] While Q shares kernels of secret knowledge with followers, that knowledge is only a starting point. The coded phrases from each drop must be carefully digested, dissected, and combined with other statements and world events in order to properly understand its "true meaning" and transform it into a concrete claim. All of this takes work. "Do your own research" has become a dictum for QAnon, a mantra to counter any claim, and followers do. QAnoners spend hours watching footage, combing through government reports, geolocating supposed targets, and stitching together "facts" drawn from all over the internet to form new theories. The sheer amount of information online, notes Matthew Hannah, creates the perfect conditions for this conspiracy-theory-driven labor, enabling "new paranoid permutations to appear, new threads to be pulled."[67]

In one sense, this work can be understood as a natural continuation of Web 2.0 culture, a shift in the early 2000s that invited users to move from passive consumption of content to actively generating it themselves. Rather than relying on the "gatekeepers" of mainstream media, digital tools democratized media production. Through digital platforms and social media, individuals could create their own stories, their own version of news and events. In recognition of this paradigm, *TIME* magazine designated it's Person of Year in 2006 as You. "You control the

Information Age," the blurb read, "welcome to your world."[68] While user-generated media is now a given online, the Q follower wholeheartedly embraces this philosophy of the individual media creator and takes it to its logical extreme. In a sense, each is building their own feed, their own custom timeline of events. When it comes to the truth, QAnoners adopt the motto of "do it yourself."

And it is this work—these practices of searching, watching, comparing, discussing, and revising within the context of a community—that forms one of the key hooks of the QAnon movement. As Ethan Zuckerman notes, QAnon is "radically participatory."[69] Rather than passively reading academic tomes, followers can actively pursue various clues, whether its decoding numbers from a drop or comparing geopolitical events for signs of things to come. "Everyone has something to focus on, a shared interest, and something to do" stated one game designer when analyzing the movement.[70] In fact, the sense of shared purpose and community belonging generated by this group activity is precisely why puzzles are used in other contexts like corporate team building. Before Q, individuals were powerless and confused, stuck in a mire of competing claims. Now they have agency. "She was no longer a lonely victim of a force she did not understand," paraphrased one journalist after talking to an ex-follower, "but part of a bigger community of people seeking the truth."

Q's Blend

Q's injunctions to "have faith" and "think for yourself" bring together a unique blend of faith and skepticism. On the one hand, there is a prominent theme of rationality, empiricism, critical thinking, and logical proofs. This theme discounts any belief in divine sovereignty and gestures to contemporary ideals of autonomy and self-sufficiency. The neoliberal self must trust herself, managing her own life and finding her own truths.[71] On the other hand, there is a strong theme of faith, justice, judgment, warfare, and Christian rhetoric running through Q's posts. The faithful must trust in God, maintaining their beliefs and awaiting the coming of justice. This theme evokes a kind of quasi-religious assembly, the children of light who must band together against the forces of darkness.

For the reader scrolling through Q's posts, these themes appear directly alongside each other. Eschatology and the Enlightenment are interwoven. While QAnon's novelty and the gap in research make any discussion speculative, one byproduct of this blend seems to be a strong community. Neoliberal invocations of the self are augmented with the overarching purpose and unified front of the religious right. Individuals are bound together into a moral community founded on the tropes of justice and warfare.[72] These cosmic mythologies establish a tight-knit "we" and bless their work as important and urgent. Q followers are faithful patriots, an assembly of good citizens struggling against evil forces. "United We Stand" proclaims one Q slogan. "Where We Go One, We Go All" declares another. Q regularly showcases video greetings from Q followers around the world, from Ghana to the UK and Iran (#3935, #3938, #4051). Each Q follower may have to investigate the truth for themselves, but these "independent researchers" are all carrying this task together, posting proofs back into the QAnon "hivemind" that are then discussed and built upon.[73] These practices collectively construct a shared reality and tie individuals into the #Qarmy.

QAnon's unique blend of narratives produces a compelling rhetorical vision, one not adequately captured by defining it only as a religion[74] or dismissing it as a cult.[75] Of course, QAnon is certainly not unprecedented; there are some clear historical connections to note. For one scholar, QAnon's obsession with blood, ritual, and sacrifice are updates of antisemitic blood libel conspiracy theories and the more recent "satanic panic" of the 1980s.[76] For another, Q feels like an extrapolation of the New Christian Right, with its hyperpatriotism and conflation of progressive values with sexual deviancy.[77] But these religious predecessors don't pull together all the puzzle pieces that QAnon does. QAnon borrows liberally to construct its powerful fantasy, drawing together the paranoid style with post-truth elements and combining enlightenment ideals with internet knowledge-construction.

QAnon's ability to incorporate all these elements is not just due to its role as "big tent" conspiracy theory, but stems more precisely from Q's writings. Q weaves together faith and paranoia, spirituality and secular humanism into a seamless story. Habermas asked "what is missing" in our post-secular age and suggested it might lie in a new marriage of faith and reason.[78] QAnon steps precisely into this gap. Granted, the "cross-fertilization of more 'secular' anti-government and apocalyptic conspiracy theories with more 'religious' ones" has been underway for at least three decades.[79] Yet the scale and success of this blend marks QAnon as new in degree, if not in kind. This is a story that applies powerful religious concepts like righteousness, justice, and evil to present-day political figures and events. This is a story told through the video grabs, GPS coordinates, and Twitter threads of Q. And this is a story remixed and retold through the growing community of independent QAnon researchers, who step others through their "logical thinking" with the use of screenshots, maps, and timestamps. Both the story itself, and the mechanisms of storytelling, then, stitch together a hybrid formation. This is a persuasive rhetorical vision that powerfully shapes a community's understanding of reality. Judging by the growing social and political influence of QAnon, this synthesis has proven coherent and compelling.

These insights into the persuasive power of QAnon are supported by the stories of former followers. Echoing the theme of faith, one ex-QAnoner stated that a fundamentalist Christian upbringing primed him to accept conspiracy thinking. "Theories about evil evolution, science denial and the End of the world rapture return of Christ stuff is all pretty crazy too," he stated, "there's a strong link between the two."[80] The same ex-follower also echoed the theme of skepticism and rationality. "Conspiracy thinking hooks the brain because it feels like critical thinking," he stressed, people "gain a massive ego boost in thinking they have a secret that the sheeple don't know."[81] Another ex-QAnoner explained that the command to do your own research "works to reinforce conspiracy theories while making people think they're coming to conclusion on their own, thanks to the way search engines and social media algorithms work."[82] Rather than being told what to believe, individuals are told to search for themselves—a far more powerful proposition that sees them inevitably finding media to support their view. While these testimonies are inherently anecdotal, they point to how Q's rhetoric mobilizes individuals. These stories reiterate the persuasive power of the QAnon narrative-blend and its ability to win hearts and minds.

These twin themes come together to form a rhetorical vision grounded in powerful religious narratives and a tight-knit community but also premised on post-truth ideals of questioning dogma and forging your own truth through online knowledge construction practices. This narrative blend offers one starting point for those seeking to understand QAnon and the powerful pull it exerts on followers. "The Great Awakening is not a conspiracy theory or a cult," state the authors, in their introduction to QAnon, "it is a sophisticated and coordinated information operation from within President Trump's administration to enlighten the public about the true state of affairs of the nation and the world."[83] While countering this dangerous movement is key, the first step is to understand how statements like this make sense at psychological, social, and cultural levels—how these powerful fantasies come to be internalized, endorsed, and propagated.

Converted to Q

What is the result of this process? When conveying the pull that the conspiracy theory now has on them, QAnoners draw on a cornucopia of rich images and analogies. Q is a "monster," a kind of invisible terror that "gnaws" at them day and night until they can't stand it any longer and succumb to its power.[84] But it is also a "rabbit hole," a slow descent into a warren or maze, where one reaches the end of a path only to find that it leads to more paths, more truths, more research. Some describe the movement as a "seed in their brain"; once it has taken root in their consciousness, its tendrils start snaking outwards, a poisonous creep that gradually takes over their "common sense."[85] And in a similar vein, others refer to the conspiracy theory as a kind of "mind virus with the internet as disease vector." The movement here becomes a type of plague, a contagious disease capable of rapidly transmitting from person to person and overtaking the host's normal cognitive functions.

All of these images testify to being overwhelmed by something, to becoming undone. The force of the conspiracy theory has overcome their defenses, the psychosocial ramparts they have erected to keep themselves safe and in control. These barriers have been thoroughly breached and no longer provide any protection. In fact, in many of these images, from monsters to seeds, QAnon already has access to the inner-life of the individual. It is not something "out there" that can be pointed at and defended against, but instead something more insidious, more invasive. It is close—indeed too close—evading the typical cognitive mechanisms used to evaluate statements, to judge contesting claims, to critique and dismiss ideas.

So these images look inward rather than outward. They locate the source of Q's hold as something that is internal to the subject. From viruses to monsters, there may be a kind of alien force at work here, but that power is only sustained parasitically, by drawing upon its host. Fear is one fuel source, with Q followers describing a deep-seated anxiety about the chaos and disorder in the world around them. "I try and resist but the doubts, the paranoia, it's too much" said one.[86] "I don't want to go down this path," he continued, "but my mind keeps circling back to it, no matter what I do."[87] These followers return to the same thoughts over and over, there is a restlessness and apprehension as they revisit the same scenarios.

In this sense, while the clues and codes of Q may be a catalyst, the follower's anxiety is ultimately driven by their own creativity and cognitive labor. The greater their imagination, the more vivid the depictions of political and social crisis become, the more alarming the slide into cultural debasement seems, and the more towering the figure of the "enemy" and their sick debauchery looms. Q's drops are just dotted outlines, fragmented and even amateur at times, that must be filled in with the hues and tones of specific targets and particular world events. These posts are cues that only come to life through a willing act of co-creation from Q followers. Through their cognitive participation, these fragmented and even amateurish texts swell into realistic portrayals of horror underlying the world's ills—plausible explanations as to why it exists and who is responsible.

This is a powerful process that has the potential to radically transform the self. "Over time," one follower said, "all my values changed." This is not just a piecemeal alteration of a few ideas, but instead a systematic alteration of a person's core tenets. In fact, one of the common hallmarks of QAnon stories is this sense of profound change. For some, this means veering from a vaguely left-leaning politics to the hard right. For others, it means deriding all of their prior education as propaganda. Deepseated beliefs about who they are, what matters to them, and what they should strive for are examined, and many discarded. New beliefs and a new purpose take their place.

Death and Rebirth

In his book *Thought Reform and the Psychology of Totalism*, Robert Lifton describes this conversion process as one of death and rebirth. Those in the midst of this process are subjected to relentless pressure, and this pressure aims to break down the very core of a person's being. Here we are not simply talking about superficial preferences—about switching from one political party or religion as a set of suppositions to another—but a far more systematic and intimate destruction, an annihilation of the beliefs, relations, and assumptions that once formed a stable identity. Remaking the individual starts by striking at the core of the self, at the heart of their personhood. And while this core may be mental, it is also deeply relational and emotional. Indeed, for Lifton, this is the crux of conversion. As he stresses: "This penetration by the psychological forces of the environment into the inner emotions of the individual person is perhaps the outstanding psychiatric fact of thought reform."[88]

How does this penetration take place? For Lifton, it is not something haphazard or improvised, but instead a kind of algorithm that plays out between the subject and the environment. This interaction takes the form of "a sequence of steps or operations," discrete "combinations of manipulation and response."[89] Such a description seems to blend together the emotional with the computational, two domains that are often seen as opposed or at least distinct. One is associated with intimacy and affect, desires and disorders, or sometimes even with the spirit and the soul. The other is often linked to logic and reason, to information and infrastructure, to science and the technocratic. Lifton is actually writing forty years prior and is describing a decidedly analogue process of brainwashing in prison. Yet his description seems to perfectly anticipate the rise of digital technologies and the way they shape the hearts and minds of individuals. Only quite recently has there been increased awareness of these possibilities and attention paid to their fallout, whether coming under the banner of emotional manipulation, social media critiques, content moderation, or online radicalization.

The technologies that drive QAnon conversion are not incredibly sophisticated: forum posts, streaming video, user-generated media, and others. In fact, observers have noted the strong presence of an older demographic of Q followers that can access this media despite being less tech-savvy. Yet as the stories here demonstrated, they clearly have a profoundly transformative effect. What is missing from this list of "mere" technologies is the social and emotional elements that attend them: a grand narrative, a compelling invitation to participate, and a welcoming community. These elements come together powerfully whenever material on Q is consumed, discussed, meditated on, or generated anew. And it is these moments, to use Lifton's words, that form a sequence of discrete manipulations over time. Such manipulations build upon each other; they accrete over time. And so, though they radically transform the subject, this transformation is often subliminal, going unregistered as such. So while this influence is powerful, it is a power that disappears from view. As Foucault noted, such power "reaches into the very grain of individuals, touches their bodies and inserts itself into their actions and attitudes, their discourses, learning processes and everyday lives."[90]

If this conversion to QAnon is successful, a new self is born and the old self cast off. For family and friends surrounding the convert, this rapid erasure is often compared to a kind of decay or even death. "I felt like the guy I fell in love with, and am still in love with, died," stated one. The Q follower seems to have killed off their former self: their conversation changes, their behaviors and habits shift dramatically, they appear fundamentally altered. "It's like watching a relative slowly slipping into dementia," observed one son of a recent devotee, "You don't recognize them anymore."[91] In some cases, the transformation seems to be total. None of the personality traits and endearing qualities that defined that person seem to remain. "She isn't 'my mom' anymore," declared one daughter. These family members may live in the same house with this person or even share the same bed, yet they feel fundamentally alienated from them. To these loved ones, it seems like the shell of the person remains but they have been hollowed out and remade from within. When they look at their father, their partner, their friend, they now see a stranger.

The converted self is often a more hateful self. To dismiss these followers as kooks and their beliefs as irrational would be a mistake. In waving them away, we implicitly condone the hateful ideals that are tied into many conspiracy theory beliefs. The ideas and ideologies inspired by Q are deeply tied into racism, antisemitism, xenophobia, and other prejudice. "These people check off all the bigoted boxes," stated one user, "racist (admitted white supremacists), homophobic, sexist, transphobic, xenophobic, whatever."[92] Another stated that the Q channel her boss watched "slowly turned her into a white supremacist," who claimed that the "Holocaust isn't real" and "Jews are trying to destroy white people."[93] For those who internalize these beliefs, they can manifest as outbursts of anger, verbal attacks on minorities, or even acts of physical violence and terrorism. And yet, there is still space for empathy and recovery, as the last chapter in this book will explore. Taking radicalization seriously—while sustaining a hefty measure of humanity—seems to win the best results.

Notes

1   Hoppa, "Affidavit."
2   Feeld, "Texas QAnon Supporter Used Car to Attack Strangers She Believed Were 'Pedophiles.'"

3   Feeld, "Texas QAnon Supporter Used Car to Attack Strangers She Believed Were 'Pedophiles.'"

4   Feeld, "Texas QAnon Supporter Used Car to Attack Strangers She Believed Were 'Pedophiles.'"

5   Feeld, "Texas QAnon Supporter Used Car to Attack Strangers She Believed Were 'Pedophiles.'"

6   Feeld, "Texas QAnon Supporter Used Car to Attack Strangers She Believed Were 'Pedophiles.'"

7   Johnson, "Trump Gathers with Military Leaders, Says 'Maybe It's the Calm before the Storm.'"

8   Energy.gov, "Departmental Personnel Security FAQs."

9   Zadrozny and Collins, "Who Is behind the Qanon Conspiracy?"

10   Zadrozny and Collins, "Who Is behind the Qanon Conspiracy?"

11   Beanz, "Tracy Beanz."

12   Reddit, "The Calm Before The Storm."

13   Zadrozny and Collins, "Who Is behind the Qanon Conspiracy?"

14   Stanley-Becker, "'We Are Q.'"

15   Collins, "What Is Qanon?"; LaFrance, "The Prophecies of Q"; Martineau, "The Storm Is the New Pizzagate — Only Worse."

16   Melley, *Empire of Conspiracy*, 8.

17   Tuters, Jokubauskaitė, and Bach, "Post-Truth Protest: How 4chan Cooked up the Pizzagate Bullshit."

18   Roose, "QAnon Followers Are Hijacking the #SaveTheChildren Movement."

19   North, "How #SaveTheChildren Is Pulling American Moms into QAnon."

20   Eylar, "How I Fell Down the QAnon Rabbit Hole (As Told by Those Still Inside It)."

21   van Prooijen, "Sometimes Inclusion Breeds Suspicion," 267.

22   van Prooijen and van Dijk, "When Consequence Size Predicts Belief in Conspiracy Theories"; McCauley and Jacques, "The Popularity of Conspiracy Theories of Presidential Assassination."

23   van Prooijen and Acker, "The Influence of Control on Belief in Conspiracy Theories."

24   van Prooijen, "Sometimes Inclusion Breeds Suspicion," 275.

25 Garry et al., "QAnon Conspiracy Theory," 187.

26 Anons, "Q: The Basics," 3.

27 Theweleit, *Male Fantasies*, 24.

28 Foss, *Rhetorical Criticism*, 411.

29 King, "Using Templates in the Thematic Analysis of Text."

30 Reyes, "Strategies of Legitimization in Political Discourse."

31 Spalding, "'We Must Put on the Armor of God,'" 103.

32 Barkun, *A Culture of Conspiracy*, 19.

33 Fenster, *Conspiracy Theories*, 227.

34 LaFrance, "The Prophecies of Q."

35 Ohlheiser, "Evangelicals Are Looking for Answers Online. They're Finding QAnon Instead."

36 Wilson, "Conspiracy Theories, Millennialism, and the Nation," 1.

37 Smith, "QAnon, Conspiracy Theories, and Evangelicals."

38 Argentino, "In the Name of the Father, Son, and Q."

39 Schwartz, "How One QAnon Believer Escaped The 'Grand Unified Theory Of All Conspiracy Theories.'"

40 Griffin, *Terrorist's Creed*, 24.

41 Griffin, *Terrorist's Creed*, 50.

42 Feldman, "Terrorist's Creed by Roger Griffin."

43 Jasko, LaFree, and Kruglanski, "Quest for Significance and Violent Extremism"; Kruglanski et al., "Fully Committed"; Kruglanski et al., "The Psychology of Radicalization and Deradicalization."

44 Griffin, *Terrorist's Creed*, 166.

45 This quote is from the original version, published in 1957, and was removed in subsequent versions. Cohn, *The Pursuit of the Millennium*.

46 Griffin, *Terrorist's Creed*, 50.

47 Schwartz, "How One QAnon Believer Escaped The 'Grand Unified Theory Of All Conspiracy Theories.'"

48 Tavernise, "'Trump Just Used Us and Our Fear.'"

49 Lantian et al., "Maybe Free Thinker but Not a Critical One."

50 See, "From Crumbs to Conspiracy," 67.

51 Steyerl, "A Sea of Data."

52 Zuckerman, "QAnon and the Emergence of the Unreal."

53 See, "From Crumbs to Conspiracy," 89.

54   Procházka and Blommaert, "Ergoic Framing in New Right Online Groups," 24.

55   Harambam and Aupers, "Contesting Epistemic Authority."

56   Uscinski, Klofstad, and Atkinson, "What Drives Conspiratorial Beliefs?"

57   Barkun, *A Culture of Conspiracy*, 41.

58   Kant, "Beantwortung Der Frage: Was Ist Aufklärung?," 1.

59   Wachowski and Wachowski, *The Matrix*.

60   Tavernise, "'Trump Just Used Us and Our Fear.'"

61   Schwartz, "How One QAnon Believer Escaped The 'Grand Unified Theory Of All Conspiracy Theories.'"

62   Schwartz, "How One QAnon Believer Escaped The 'Grand Unified Theory Of All Conspiracy Theories.'"

63   Engels, *The Politics of Resentment*, 34.

64   Engels, *The Politics of Resentment*, 34.

65   Schwartz, "How One QAnon Believer Escaped The 'Grand Unified Theory Of All Conspiracy Theories.'"

66   Lalich, *Bounded Choice*, 74.

67   Hannah, "QAnon and the Information Dark Age."

68   Grossman, "You—Yes You—are TIME's Person of the Year."

69   Zuckerman, "QAnon and the Emergence of the Unreal."

70   Berkowitz, "A Game Designer's Analysis Of QAnon."

71   Gershon, "Neoliberal Agency."

72   Graham and Haidt, "Beyond Beliefs."

73   Zuckerman, "QAnon and the Emergence of the Unreal."

74   Argentino, "In the Name of the Father, Son, and Q."

75   Stanley-Becker, "'We Are Q.'"

76   Lavin, "QAnon, Blood Libel, and the Satanic Panic"; on blood libel, see Rose, *The Murder of William of Norwich*.

77   Goodwin, QAnon Didn't Just Spring Forth From the Void — It's the Latest From a Familiar Movement.

78   Habermas, *An Awareness of What Is Missing*.

79   Stroop, "Behind a Recent Stunt in Idaho Lies a Dangerous Theocratic Movement."

80 Diceblue, "R/QAnonCasualties—I'm an Ex Q, Former Conspiracy Theorist, Ama."

81 Diceblue, "R/QAnonCasualties—I'm an Ex Q, Former Conspiracy Theorist, Ama."

82 Reneau, "A Former QAnon Believer Answers All Your Questions about How the Cult Really Works."

83 Anons, "Q: The Basics," 6.

84 qstruggling, "Going Crazy."

85 qstruggling, "Trouble Moving On."

86 qstruggling, "Going Crazy."

87 qstruggling, "Going Crazy."

88 Lifton, *Thought Reform and the Psychology of Totalism*, 144.

89 Lifton, *Thought Reform and the Psychology of Totalism*, 144.

90 Foucault, "Prison Talk," 39.

91 BlackPoseidon, "Dad Is Too Far Gone, Thinks I'm Possessed by a Demon."

92 deleted, "It's Really Only a Matter of Time until I Become Estranged with Q Family and I Just Wonder When It's Gonna Come."

93 sumterwinner, "Boss and Job."

Parler's Patriotic Hate

2:28pm, Capitol Building, Washington, D.C. The video provides a panoramic view of the chaos below. On the left side of the frame are the steps leading up to the East entrance, occupied by clusters of police. They are decked out in full black riot gear, armored up with plexiglas helmets, shields, and steel batons. And yet they seem disorganized and clearly overwhelmed, unsure of how to respond.

On the right side of the frame are thousands of protestors. When panning across this sea of bodies, what springs to the eye first are the flags. Dotted across the crowd is the well-known red, white, and blue hues of the Star Spangled Banner. But intermingled with this flag are Make America Great Again flags and Trump 2020 flags, proclaiming allegiance to a particular commander-in-chief, the distinctive red and black Confederate flag, with its ominous ties to antebellum slavery, the bright yellow Gadsden flag, with its curling serpent as symbol of anti-government sentiment, the 3 Percenter flag, the banner of a far-right militia who falsely claim that 3% of Americans fought against the British, and here and there, the green Kek flag, a spoof of the Nazi war flag with allusions to Pepe the Frog concocted somewhere deep in the bowels of 4chan.

In the middle of the frame is a row of metal fences erected as a temporary barricade. A dozen officers stand behind them, but already this defense seems flimsy, precarious. We see a crush of bodies building up behind them, jostling, shoving, pushing. A final swell ripples in from the right and the dam breaks, rioters tossing aside portions of the fence. A roar rises from the crowd, and a stream of bodies plows through the gap and onto the steps. Some individuals turn back to the crowd, motioning for them to advance. A police officer tries to stop the crowd from advancing up the steps, only to be viciously body-checked from behind and topple over the rail. The red mist of pepper spray drifts over the steps, but the crowd shrugs it off, barreling up to the door leading to the Rotunda. The police, already lacking any semblance of coordination, mill around, fending off direct attacks but mostly watching as clusters of people wrapped in flags or kitted out in camouflage file past.

Once the breach is made, the crowd quickly floods into the ground floors of the Rotunda, tramping through the stately hallways with their marble floors and ornate decorations. In one video posted at 2:37pm, a man picks up a telephone, miming a call: "Nancy Pelosi? Yeah we're coming for you bitch. Oh Mike Pence? We're coming for you too fucking traitor." In another, we see a cluster of people hounding a security guard, who retreats up the stairs. Later it was discovered that he was intentionally leading the crowd away from the debating chamber, where politicians had been meeting to ratify the result of the presidential elections.

2:42pm, we follow a man traipsing down a carpeted hallway of offices. As others kick against the locked doors, he starts up a chant, belting out "defend your constitution, defend your liberty" over and over on a megaphone. At the same moment, a cluster of rioters below the Rotunda break out in a chorus of the Battle Hymn of the Republic. "Glory, Glory Hallelujah," they sing, "His truth is marching on." The camera is placed on the floor, looking directly up into the painted mosaic on the ceiling, a Renaissance lookalike depicting white figures dressed in robes. A cluster of rioters kneel down in spontaneous prayer. "God thank you for letting us stand up for our country and what we believe in. Guide us so we may do Your will. I pray for that and I pray for these brothers that stand beside me. In the name of Jesus, Amen."

At 2:51pm, a man turns to face the camera in a moment of introspection: "What is it going to take, if the election is being stolen?" he asks, "is it going to take just people talking about it?" "Talk is cheap," he concludes, "and if this is going to make me lose my job, then so be it. I don't care about my reputation, I care about my nation. There comes a point where you have to *do*." At 4:57pm, we pan across a trashed office, with furniture upended and figures standing around. A woman's voice, clearly the one filming, utters a statement with absolute conviction: "I will die for this country."

On 6 January 2021, a violent mob stormed the United States Capitol. Driven by a shared belief that the U.S. election was stolen, the group attempted to disrupt the formalization of Joe Biden's presidential victory. To get inside the building, the group overran barricades, smashed windows, and attacked police. The formalization session was halted and both the Senate and House were evacuated, with members donning gas masks to protect them from tear gas. Once inside, rioters roamed around the Senate floor, live-streaming their actions and taking selfies, while police barricaded the House chamber and prepared to defend it at gunpoint. Five individuals were killed, including one officer who died from being bludgeoned with a fire extinguisher. The footage described above comes from this event, a fraction of the full set of 500 clips depicting selfies and shattered glass, crowds and conflict, grand spectacles and small moments. All of these videos were posted by users of one social-media platform: Parler.

* * *

In this chapter, I explore patriotic hate, using the lens of Parler and the Capitol Storming to focus the investigation. As in the rest of the book, I'm interested in seeing how digital structures and affordances shape the psyche at both the individual and collective levels. How do network technologies amplify the draw of white nationalism and its motivational intensity in the hearts and minds of individuals? Drawing on race studies and political theory, I'll argue that the rising progressivism of the last decade (even if symbolic or partial), produced loss and confusion in the white subjects who considered themselves to be the racial core of the nation. The result was a deep sense of disorientation.

In the midst of this uncertainty, white nationalism is a rock, a compelling story offering a reason for this mess and a way back to dignity. Those who embrace this framing are patriots, the rightful heirs of the nation who must safeguard it with violence if necessary. Those who disagree with this vision are tyrants, who must be condemned and undermined in every possible way. While white nationalism is a longstanding and diverse ideology, I'm particularly interested in how it becomes updated and operationalized through networked media. How do the affordances of digital platforms sustain and amplify these racialized myths? Parler provides an example of what I call "operational media," offering subjects an action, a reason to do it, and a plan for carrying it out. Operational media takes simmering white resentment and scaffolds it into a shared vision and a specific program.

The First White President

Platforms like Parler do not come from nowhere, but instead emerge from a simmering pool of racialized politics and historical whiteness. To understand Parler and the storming of the Capitol, we need to understand what came before it. In the next few sections, then, I dive into the conditions that produced the user base of these platforms and the drive to conduct violence on behalf of the nation, the prerequisites that fomented the hate to come.

Trump's election in 2016 is one critical moment that established these conditions, an event that shocked the world. For many commentators, Trump's surprising presidential victory could be explained as the revenge of the white working class. These ordinary, hardscrabble Americans had been sneered at and patronized by Washington elites for years. They had searched for someone to represent their basic needs—a steady job, a steady economy, and so on—but were presented by a non-choice of wealthy politicians beholden to corporate interests. As a result, they voted for Trump as the anti-politician, a populist champion who would clear out "the swamp" of status-quo politics with all its corruption and start afresh by reasserting the needs of working-class people.

But as Ta-Nehisi Coates argues in the "First White President," working class resentment as the sole driver of Trump's success obscures a much more troubling explanation. What Trump demonstrated—and deftly tapped into—was a deep vein of whiteness and anxiety at the core of national politics. He grasped that this stratum of racialized resentment had been buried rather than eradicated, and that it could be mined for tremendous political power. Certainly the tenets at the heart of antebellum slavery had been taken up and deployed by politicians, often to great success, over decades. Yet in the recent past, this rhetoric had been coded, using veiled phrases like "welfare queens," "gangbangers," or "illegal immigrants" to conjure up stereotypes and slogans like "tough on crime" to appeal to a certain demographic. As Ian Haney-López notes, this "dog whistle politics" leveraged race while always insisting that race was irrelevant.[1] Racism was an ugly relic of the past; in the post-racial present, it should never influence a candidate's principles or platforms. Despite such protests, audiences excelled at reading between the lines, latching onto the unstated targets of campaign speeches and policy initiatives.

Trump dispensed with these dog whistles and their veneer of respectability. His campaign kicked off by endorsing the birther conspiracy, the false claim that Obama was born in Kenya and not the United States, making him ineligible to run for the presidency. From there it only become more virulent. Mexicans were "rapists" bringing drugs and crime into the country. Haiti and African countries were "shithole countries." Muslims hated the U.S. One of his political opponents was smeared with antisemitic imagery that alleged she was the "most corrupt candidate ever." In another tweet, he labeled an opposing candidate "Pocahontas" and said he'd see her on "the trail."

If Trump has openly denigrated other races, he has been just as overt with his championing of whiteness. When asked to comment on the Unite the Right rally in Charlottesville, where white supremacists carried tiki torches and killed a counter protestor by ramming into a crowd with a car, Trump famously stated that "both sides" were to blame for the violence and that there were "some very fine people" amongst the white supremacists. And when challenged in a presidential debate to publicly condemn organized white hate groups like the Proud Boys, Trump instead told them to "stand back and standby," a message that was interpreted by the group as a sign of support or even need. Whether as speeches or tweets, this show of support for white values has energized white supremacist movements and organizations. "The success of the Trump campaign just proves that our views resonate with millions," stated one representative of the Knights party, the successor of the KKK.[2] While these elements have always been around, Trump's statements have made them bolder, more strident. White supremacy no longer needs to be whispered behind closed doors; it has already been shouted through a microphone from the podium.

The strategy was a success, and not just with working class folks. The polls clearly show that Trump's grip on the nation extended far beyond that particular demographic. As Coates observes: "Trump won white women (+9) and white men (+31). He won white people with college degrees (+3) and white people without them (+37). He won young whites, age 18 to 29 (+4), adult whites, age 30 to 44 (+17), middle-age whites, age 45 to 64 (+28), and senior whites, age 65 and older (+19). According to Edison Research, Trump won whites in midwestern Illinois (+11), whites in mid-Atlantic Maryland (+12), and whites in sunbelt New Mexico (+5)...if you only tallied the popular vote of "white America" to derive 2016 electoral votes, Trump would defeat Clinton 389 to 81, with the remaining 68 votes either a "toss-up" or unknown."[3]

The racialized sentiment driving these results was not confined to some narrow band of blue-collar workers or southern rednecks. These voters come from the heartland but also from the coasts with their cosmopolitan associations. They hail from the Rust Belt and its postindustrial towns, but also the Bible Belt, with their farming communities and religious values. These are college students and retirees, rural poor but also wealthy urbanites. They range enormously in their age and level of education. This diverse pool of people, with its heterogeneous mix of backgrounds, socioeconomic, and life stages, spills far over the container of "working class," however broadly defined. What unites this broad base is something at once more simple and more disconcerting: they are all white.

That Trump was able to mobilize this broad church of voters points to a troubling truth. Racial prejudice is not some vestige from the past that has been overcome in a bright new era of progressivism. It is not some backwards mindset held by a small niche of backwards people. No, racist beliefs are alive and well, thriving in the hearts and minds of mainstream

Americans. In that sense, Trump's strategy is not novel, but a reversion or a repetition. It is telling that Martin Luther King's observation from fifty years ago perfectly captures the contemporary moment: "the white backlash is nothing new," he stressed, "It is the surfacing of old prejudices, hostilities, and ambivalences that have always been there."[4] Structures of white power were always present, bunkered deep into the political landscape. It was only a matter of recognizing them, picking them up, and fashioning them into a weapon.

And yet this reality is too stark to be confronted, too disturbing to be faced head on. Political commentators bury their heads in the sand, pointing instead to a downtrodden working class, a group of industrious individuals who have been short-changed by economic shifts and elitist politics. This tale helps to ease our conscience and prop up a post-racial myth, to explain away the more troubling truth that the polls tell. "The implications," writes Coates, "that systemic bigotry is still central to our politics, that the country is susceptible to that bigotry, that the salt-of-the-earth Americans whom we lionize in our culture and politics are not so different from those same Americans who grin back at us in lynching photos… are just too dark."[5] The next section rewinds the clock to sketch out this reality.

White Nationalism as Operating System

These racialized structures were present at the birth of the nation. "The United States has always been a racial state," argues Moon-Kie Jung, "a state of white supremacy."[6] The decision of the colonies to declare independence was driven by freedom. But as Jung notes, that freedom was principally the freedom to carry out colonization and western expansion without being shackled by their mother country. Written into this settler colonialism was the logic of white superiority, a logic that reduced blacks to subhuman status, chattels that could be made to work, and Native American land to wilderness that needed to be violently cleared of its savage inhabitants. From free labor to free land, there were clear benefits to be had from embracing this logic, lucrative advantages that set up cycles of generational wealth. Such a logic, then, was not arbitrary, but calculating, a strategic move that awarded its advocates concrete benefits. As Steve Martinot stresses, these material gains were the original "interest" that drove the consolidation of the colonial regime.[7]

This logic did not emerge by accident, but was carefully coded over time. To explore this development, we can turn to the work of Chip Berlet and Matthew Lyons. In the early colonies, the duo explain, a good proportion of both white and black settlers worked in indentured servitude or bond-service, giving them similar status and working conditions. In 1676 Nathaniel Bacon leveraged this shared plight into an armed rebellion against the Colonial Governor. Disturbed by this alliance between Europeans and Africans, the British regime quickly moved to formalize the status of particular subjects and reassert a distinct caste hierarchy. The result, as Berlet and Lyons note, was that the "colonial elite drove a wedge between the two laboring groups: reducing Africans from the ambiguous status of bond-service to permanent, hereditary slavery, and elevating Europeans over them with a system of legal and social privileges based on skin color and ancestry."[8] This codified difference not only created a distinction between black and white, but established the former as inferior and the latter as superior.

From there, the authors trace a lineage of populism rooted in white supremacy, moving from Thomas Paine's best-selling *Common Sense* that claimed that the British were "barbarous and hellish power, which hath stirred up the Indians and Negroes to destroy us," to the Naturalization Law of 1790 that limited citizenship to "free white persons," the Indian Removal Act of 1830 that forced large groups of Native Americans to migrate, and the Republican Party's early slogan of itself as the "white man's party." Through these events, Berlet and Lyon aim to show that repressive populism is not "extremist," but rather part of mainstream political thought that has long been at the heart of the nation. In fact, the duo's genealogy is much longer, stretching from the colonial era through to the Jacksonians and the Reagan administration. Yet I list these early events because they powerfully link the genesis of the nation to a certain conception of "the people."

One of the defining features of this populism is its producerist ideology. In this tale, "the people" are the producers, everyday people who work hard and add real value to society. In a fair world, they would be rewarded for their dedication and contribution. But instead, they find themselves beaten down and disenfranchised. Two groups are to blame for this predicament. The first are the "elite parasites from above," government bureaucrats, Jews, bankers, and so on. The second are the "lazy and sinful parasites from below," people of color, immigrants, homosexuals, and so on. Whether through liberalism or laziness, these parasites are dragging down the economic and moral fabric of society. These blood suckers are siphoning off the prosperity that should be rightfully theirs.

What, then, is the solution? While different movements proposed different solutions, they all involve a degree of exclusion—propping up the rights and privileges of that select group who gets to call themselves "the people" while marginalizing and punishing those (legally, financially, physically) who are considered to be outside of it. Already we can see how this "narrative package" employing "demonization, scapegoating, and conspiracism" offers a powerful but flexible framework.[9] It establishes a crystal-clear hierarchy based on supposed merit, with the producers at the apex. These producers are only asking for "what they deserve," but those just rewards are being pilfered before their very eyes by lesser groups. This tale stirs up a sense of righteous indignation, of being wronged. In this sense it is capable of mobilizing deep affective forces from individual and groups. But there is also a flexibility to this framework, an ability to adapt it to new situations and contexts. In the genealogy laid out by Berlet and Lyon, we see each new political movement grasping this tool and adjusting it to their needs. Each new group inserted themselves into the role of the producerists, hard-working and deserving of reward, while new enemies—from Jews to Catholics to people of color—were slotted into the roles of parasites from above and below.

Taken together, these texts and events testify to a powerful double-pronged idea embedded at the core of the nation's history: the nation belongs to the people—and "the people" can be defined as needed. For white nationalists, the people will always be defined in the same way, as a racial core of white Europeans. By making this claim, they insist they are irreplaceable, that they possess an "enduring right to dominion."[10] In this sense, they are not interested in democracy. Democracy only works when change is accepted—sometimes your party wins, sometimes it loses. It means yielding to the fact that the power that had once seemed so tightly tied to your group and their interests can be wrested from your grasp. And it also means acknowledging that the demographics of the nation can shift. The racial, cultural, and ethnic makeup of the country will inevitably change over time. White ethnonationalism rejects this change, asserting that they are a historically hegemonic group who alone comprise "the people." They have ruled; they now rule; they will always rule.

White nationalism, then, has long been the operating system at the heart of this nation, the source code upon which many of its systems and institutions are built upon. Understanding this racial "software" developed over two hundred years helps us to understand modern day digital platforms like Parler that leverage it. With this legacy in mind, we can better grasp the ideologies and motivations of radical right users. We can trace thick lines from the past to the present. In 1927, Albert Johnson from the House of Representatives asserted: "our capacity to maintain our cherished institutions stands diluted by a stream of alien blood, with all its inherited misconceptions respecting the relationships of the governing power to the governed."[11] In 2017, white nationalists marched through Charlottesville carrying tiki torches and chanted: "you will not replace us." And in 2021, Parler users swarmed to the top of the U.S. Capitol steps, faced the sea of white faces and American flags, and shouted: "this is our house, this is not their house." These statements, and others like them, emerge from the same core logic. Separated by time, they seek to accomplish the same operation: claiming the nation for a white citizenry and insisting that they as "the people" should always manage and control it.

For the white nationalist, these rights were coded into the nation, and so they have and will always apply. When they sense this logic being rewritten—undone by progressives, queers, people of color, and so on—they will intervene to restore a previous version of the operating system. This is the revisionism behind statements like "make America great again." And yet, as the slogan's "make" suggests, this return to former things also offers a compelling goal for what should come next. Only by restoring the original source code can we build a viable future. This is the logic of white nationalism and the logic of many who participated in the Capitol storming. It is the same logic we see in the infamous 14 words coined by white supremacist David Lane: "We must secure the existence of our people and a future for white children."

White Loss, White Rage

For those who join platforms like Parler, it's clear that white nationalism as an operating system is being gradually overwritten, recoded with different values and variables at its core. Here we want to zoom in on the individual, moving from the grand sweep of "ideology" to the more personal level of psychology. What does it feel like to understand oneself and the nation in this way, to believe that your role at the center of political power is being eroded, day after day, and that this powerlessness is causing a once-great nation to slide into decadence and decline? On Parler and other social media sites, the phrase "Stop the Steal" has quickly risen to prominence, a phrase referring to Trump being "cheated" out of re-election by fraudulent machines, fraudulent voters, and a fraudulent system. Yet if this hashtag refers to the loss of an election, its totemic power also seems drawn from a broader sense of deprivation—the loss of economic security, the loss of racial dignity, the loss of "our" nation to "them."

In an essay on melancholic nationalism, Michael Feola notes that the trauma for the white subject is not just that these social, cultural, and political advantages are "slipping away," but that they are being actively "taken by undeserving others."[12] In essence, this narrative is a variation of the Great Replacement Theory we saw in Chapter 2. Whether through charitable immigration schemes at the border, diversity initiatives in the workplace, critical race theory at the university, or political correctness in everyday life, the bundle of privileges once enjoyed by the white subject is being snatched in front of their eyes and divvied out to "them"—blacks,

Asians, Latinx people, migrants, queers, progressives, "globalists," and other out-groups. What is lost and who it is lost to may vary. But the logic is consistent: the white subject is being robbed of what is rightfully theirs.

Of course, this loss is perceived rather than real. Systems still employ forms of racial discrimination, privileging white subjects. We might think here of racial profiling in policing, of deep-seated prejudices in the prison system, of algorithmic bias in search engines, or of selective hiring practices in human resources—all of which have been documented by researchers or investigative journalists. "The *actual* displacement of white normativity is questionable at best and highly doubtful at worst," stress Gray, Finley, and Martin, "virtually all of the public institutions remain oriented around epistemological, ontological, social, and religious efforts at maintaining whiteness's significance as a norm."[13] The feeling that whites' position in the world is rapidly declining, that the social, cultural, and political capital that previously flowed to them is being cut off, is just that—a feeling. Disenfranchisement is a state of mind rather than an accurate reflection of reality.

Even if this loss were real, there should be nothing to grieve. White nationalism goes hand in hand with barbarism. The "racial contract" at the heart of the settler colonial state, and the advantages it offered to its chosen subjects, could only be maintained through systemic violence. Prosperity and autonomy for some was built upon the subjugation and slavery of others. Dismantling these systems and slowly pushing towards equality (however incremental or partial) should be welcomed.

Yet such concessions can never be registered in the worldview of replacement theory. One of the defining traits of whiteness, notes philosopher George Yancy, is that it allows subjects to speak from an "invisible (or unacknowledged) center."[14] Whiteness never needs to draw attention to itself, to crassly voice its claims out loud. It is not a concrete thing that can be pointed to, but rather something ambient or even atmospheric, silent suffusing through the structures and relations of our institutions. As Ahmed observes, the phenomenology of whiteness is lived as the "background to experience,"[15] an element that is always there but never the focal point.

Whiteness never needs to be named or openly declared—and it is precisely this breeziness, this effortlessness, that underpins much of its power. This invisibility cloaks itself even from those who wield it. As Mills notes, a key component of the racial contract is an "epistemology of ignorance" in which "whites are unable to understand the world that they themselves have made."[16] The white subject is blissfully unaware of the long history of injustice that places her in her position. When it comes to the network of disparities needed to sustain her privilege, she gets to be clueless. After all, one of the privileges of being white is not having to know.

All of this means that, even if replacement theory is mistaken, it still possesses real force. White anxiety about non-white progress is irrational and unfounded, but still registers as anxiety. As Arlie Hochschild stresses, this is a story of anger and mourning, a "feels-as-if" story that bypasses judgment and fact.[17] For the white subject, the shock and sense of loss is tangible. Having stood atop the social hierarchy for so long, the loss of stature is not just a step down, but a kind of tumble into the abyss. The assumptions of the past give way in their hands. The nation no longer seems recognizable. The news and media seem unexplainable. The sense of deprivation and disorientation is real. For this reason, merely dismissing these feelings or the racialized worldview that produces them is not enough. As Feola warns, such approaches "do not sufficiently engage the motivational depth of white melancholia, the distinct forms of political subjectivity forged by loss, or the politics that stems from melancholic rage."[18]

Parler Rises

White loss and white rage set the stage for the birth of Parler—even if those affective elements are buried in layers of technical specifications and business models. Launched in mid 2018 by two computer-science graduates from Denver, the platform initially remained fairly small and quiet. But that changed six months later, in December, when a conservative commentator tweeted about it. 40,000 users hit the platform at once, causing a huge spike in traffic that temporarily knocked the servers offline. In the following months, a number of big names joined the platform, from Trump lawyer Rudy Giuliani and Trump campaign manager Brad Parscale to right-wing commentators like Laura Loomer and Milo Yiannopoulos, and the founder of the Proud Boys, Gavin McInnes.[19]

In response, the Parler team quickly pivoted from their original "bipartisan" model to explicitly courting conservative influencers and organizations.[20] In fact, these unbiased aspirations may have always been a facade. In 2020 it was revealed that Rebekah Mercer, the heiress and prominent conservative donor, was the lead investor for the platform, bankrolling its development and expansion.[21] Such deep pockets come with political strings attached, as the platform's CEO found when he was fired by the company's Mercer-controlled board two years later.[22] These details on the financial backing of the platform are not simply trivia, but point to its purpose, its raison d'être. For those who control and maintain it, Parler was never merely a technical alternative to social media, but instead a hinge for political power. The prime directive was to construct a digital nexus uncontrolled by progressive interests, a space able to draw together disparate right-wing and conservative groups into a critical mass of voices that could not be "silenced."

Parler has grown extraordinarily over the last few years, a growth that can be tracked in detail thanks to the work of researchers at Stanford Internet Observatory.[23] In mid 2019, 200,00 pro-government accounts from Saudi Arabia joined, citing censorship from mainstream social media companies, a major influx that quickly doubled the existing user base. In mid 2020, the platform experienced another surge as the populist leader of Brazil, Jair Bolsonaro, and his followers joined the platform, putting the number of total users around the 3 million mark. These international cohorts gesture to the ways in which populism becomes globalized and adapted for different contexts. But the greatest spike by far came in the wake of the U.S. Presidential election in November 2020. Over just three months, the user base skyrocketed from 4 million to roughly 13 million accounts. Surging in downloads, it briefly occupied the top spot on the App store, with its CEO stating it was adding millions of users to its user base.[24]

At its core, Parler is a Twitter clone without the Twitter censorship, a platform that promises to let its users "speak free." And yet in practice, "speaking free" has often meant speaking in racist, sexist, or derogatory terms about the enemy. Parler is widely understood to be a hate haven, a place where ardent Trump supporters mix with individuals and organizations associated with the far-right and alt-right. As mainstream social networks like Facebook and Twitter came under increased pressure to regulate content, these kinds of users found themselves being blocked, suspended, or banned altogether. In the midst of this "Great Purge," Parler became a kind of lifeboat for the radical right, welcoming them onto the platform and promising never to censor their posts. Over the last two years, a number of prominent individuals and organizations have migrated to Parler, including politicians such as Ted Cruz,[25] QAnon conspiracy theorists,[26] influencers like Fox News hosts Mark Levin and Sean Hannity, and overtly violent groups like the Boogaloo movement.[27] By the end of 2020, with the Capitol Storming just a week away, Parler had accumulated a dense mixture of pro-Trumpians, religious fundamentalists, anti-government elements, and militant organizations, a critical mass of people that would place the platform in a unique position.

Storming the Capitol

There are many ways to approach Parler and the storming of the Capitol, but in this chapter I'm interested most in how it scaffolds thoughts and actions. White nationalism, even if powerful, is a broad ideology that might suggest any number of responses. White rage, despite its affective grip, is unfocused and ambient, landing variously on one scapegoat and then another. And even Trump's rallies and speeches, while certainly a factor, were vague, giving his followers a general command to "fight like hell" and "take back our country." His rhetoric, while antagonistic, was limited in its specifics by the norms of public office. What exactly should be the agenda of this war and its potential targets? How might it be legitimated and its combatants understood? And besides Trump, what goals and ideals did these disparate followers share? White nationalism provides orientation and a sense of belonging, but it is insufficient by itself.

Over the next few sections, I show how digital media augments white nationalism, taking its overarching tenets or principles and operationalizing them. Operational media sharpens broad principles into concrete targets; it channels free-floating grievance into specific plans. Media reports described the group attacking the Capitol as a mob. But if a mob is dangerous, it can also be unstable and directionless, assembling for a moment but accomplishing nothing. I am interested, then, in how Parler worked at logistical, organizational, and ideological levels to render this public into a more stabilized and cohesive force. Through the affordances of the platform—feeds, groups, and messages—this group had already singled out certain enemies and playtested particular scenarios. This media scaffolding allowed the intense anger mobilized at the rallies to be folded into an actionable plan.

Parler's role as a hyper-conservative platform and the makeup of its user base gives it strong connections to the 6 January attack. But even more specifically, GPS metadata associated with Parler posts showed how its users "breached deep inside" the U.S. Capitol.[28] The videos described in the introduction to this chapter are just a fraction of the hundreds of clips posted from the hallways, offices, and stairwells of the Capitol building. As Parler's formative role in the storming of the Capitol became clearer, its Web host, Amazon Web Services, announced it would terminate services to the platform in a matter of days.[29] During this period, a number of researchers and activists, led by hacker "donk_enby,"[30] scrambled to collect the thousands of posts and videos that had been recently published, hoping to gain a comprehensive portrait of activity leading up to the event before it was taken offline indefinitely.

As a result of that work, a computer science researcher collected approximately 350,000 posts written or shared in the days prior to and including the attack and made them freely available to others.[31] My analysis draws on that data. From an ethical perspective, it should be noted that this material was obtained by Web scraping, a legal method used to obtain text and images from publicly accessible Web pages through batch requests. I also never identify authors of posts, either through their username or real name. For these reasons, and to avoid directing traffic to a platform like Parler, posts are never formally cited or hyperlinked.

Methodologically, I use a theoretical sampling approach, "identifying emergent concepts in data being generated which are then used to guide where, how and from whom more data should be collected, and with what focus."[32] Rather than coding or classifying each of these 350,000 posts, I adopted a consciously exploratory rather than systematic approach, drawing on my domain expertise in online hate, radical right cultures, and conspiracy theory to identify salient themes within this material and then use the same author or similar keywords to thicken these themes with additional examples. This approach follows one of the principal aims of theoretical sampling in seeking to build and refine theory from data.[33]

Mobilizing

Operational media mobilizes. "CALLING ALL PATRIOTS," reads one post with over 50,000 impressions, "DONALD TRUMP HAS CALLED FOR US TO COME TO THE NATIONS CAPITOL FOR THE LAST STAND AGAINST THE GLOBALISTS." There is a simple logistical function at work here, circulating the location and date where participants should assemble. And yet these posts also serve as identifying markers, establishing both the stakes and the sides. In the example above, the battle is between "the patriots" and "the globalists," a conflict framed in urgent terms as a "last stand." Given this identity-constructing role, even mundane posts documenting the journey towards this event also work to knit participants together. "God bless America! Patriots singing on flight to DC" reads one post. Another post recounts how politician Mitt Romney boarded one flight to D.C. "filled with Patriots who Chanted Traitor and Grilled Him About Ties to Biden." The participants have not yet congregated; the rally is still days away; but already these posts are working to generate a sense of shared purpose and social cohesion.

Part of this function is stabilization. As a collective ideology, white nationalism has deep roots and a long-term duration. It has endured and will endure. But as an emotional or psychological response on an individual level, white loss and white rage can be ephemeral, fluctuating with moods or personal experiences. This is the same "rage supply" problem we encountered in the Chapter on 8chan. Media steps in to fix this rage in place or even to amplify it. Media acts as a form of memory, drawing thoughts out of the collective and inscribing them into concrete forms: texts, messages, images, or videos. Fleeting thoughts are transformed into digital bits that are stored indefinitely on a server. This technical transformation is also psychological in acting as a form of external memory. Toxic ideas about race, class, and gender can be recalled and repeated, invoked once more in the mind of a reader. The individual is reminded, over and over again, precisely why a group is inferior, or evil, or less than human. Transient rage is converted to more durable hate. Social media, of course, adds a new wrinkle to this dynamic with its mechanisms of distribution. This is less a diary, where individual thoughts are written down and repeated, and more a form of broadcast media, where claims can quickly fan out in a matter of seconds to networks around the world. Popular posts and images go far beyond individual storage and repetition and become something more like contagion, influencing the thoughts of hundreds, thousands, or even millions of other people.

So if "us" and "them" are becoming more defined, the definition of "us" is also enlarging. On networked media, one of the primary ways this is accomplished is through the hashtag. Far more than a piece of metadata or a semantic marker, the hashtag provides a way to forge temporary publics.[34] One post, with 65,000 impressions, shows how this can be done:

Calm before the storm Get Ready Patriots
#WomenForTrump #MagaMarchDC #MAGA2021 #TRUMP #TRUMP2021
#HoldTheLine #maga #donaldtrump #Marchfortrump #DC #whitehouse #stopthestealcaravan #ElectionFruad #HoldTheLinePatriots
#WashingtonDC #trumptrain #Teamtrump #protest #4moreyears
#mmmdc12 #stormtheCapital #patriotsunited #patriots #magamarch

#millionmagamarch2021 #trumprally #proudboys #ProudboysUSA
#fuckAntifa #parler #parlerusa #trumpmarch #fakeelection #fake-
elections #fakepolls #stopthesteal #millionmagamarch #dcprotest
#dcprotests #rightwing #Stopthesteal2021 #jan6 #jan6th #wildprotest
#MillionMAGA #theproudboys

On one level, this post is simply exploiting the logic of the hashtag to
amplify the reach of its message on social media. Yet if these hashtags
work to surface the post to different communities, they also function
to stitch those communities together, to construct a collective identity.
These tags are bridges between camps, asserting that, despite their obvious differences, there are some common ideals and shared interests.
Whether contesting a "stolen election" or countering the nefarious plans
of "Antifa," multiple groups believe they must "#HoldTheLine." The post
draws on these types of synergies to expand its potential public. This
event will not just be one that matters to a niche public of Trump supporters, but to a broader coalition of "patriots," a "big tent" composed
of protestors, election conspiracists, Q-followers, Proud Boys, and anti-
Antifa activists.

Posts like these demonstrate how radical right interests have in-
novatively leveraged networked media to attract a broader audience.
These platforms mobilize users by marking out a position halfway between the mainstream Web and what we might term the sewer Web.
The mainstream Web is composed of the social media behemoths of
Facebook, Instagram, Twitter, and others. This bright arena is highly
accessible but also highly controlled in policing behaviors and language.
The sewer Web, by contrast, is made up of legacy hate havens like 4chan
and 8kun and encrypted messaging platforms like Telegram. These environments are highly creative but often overwhelming and confusing
spaces where shock humor, disturbing imagery, and manga lore sit
side by side—and explicit violence and child porn are only a click away.
Parler, Gab, and other "Alt-tech"[35] platforms offer a midpoint between
these extremes. These are accessible spaces that emulate the look-and-
feel of mainstream platforms, offering users an intuitive experience. At
the same time, they promise a more unconstrained experience, where

"censorship" imposed by corporate platforms has been reduced to a minimum.[36] The content circulating in these spaces, then, often oscillates between reasoned hyper-conservatism and more strident incitements to violence, between barely suppressed racism and explicit racial slurs, between political mudslinging and personal death threats (see the chapter on Gab for more on this). These platforms form a "bridging function between an established conservatism and an explicitly anti-democratic, latently or openly violent right-wing extremism."[37]

Parler users employ the novel affordances of social media to fashion a networked public,[38] temporarily bringing together an array of pro-Trumpian voices to form an imagined collective. And yet rather than merely remaining "networked," "mediated," or "imagined," as this language might suggest, the diversity of the 6 January crowd, ranging from military vets to real estate moms, demonstrated that such preparatory media has material consequences in the "real world." Numerous articles in the wake of the storming noted how the offline had moved online.[39] But the visceral and tragic events that took place on that day question whether that distinction still makes any sense. As everyday life becomes increasingly mediated, operational media works ahead of political events, shaping the makeup and expectations of the publics who attend. Boots on the ground are preempted by boots on the platform.

Inciting

Second, operational media incites participants towards violent action. "People do not commit political violence without discourse," notes David Apter, "they need to talk themselves into it."[40] Violence, in this sense, is a kind of threshold that must be incrementally attained, a moral and psychological boundary that must be worked towards. Radical and particularly far-right actors on platforms deploy a deluge of media that aims to move its audience closer towards this boundary over time. While wide-ranging in its messages and level of explicitness, this media shares a common logic: to stir up antagonisms, to aggravate and inflame them, and to constantly intensify this animosity to the point where it must erupt into violent action. If the mobilizing rhetoric discussed above worked to establish the boundaries of "us" and "them," these kinds of challenges do the same, asking the real "patriots" to step forward and deeply commit while others stand on the sidelines.

One strategy for inciting violence is to drive a wedge between talking and doing, between symbolic gestures and transformative deeds. To this end, a number of posts in the Parler corpus stressed the difference between empty posturing and real action. "Just protesting is going to change the minds of the socialist marxist Democrat asshole's who have stolen our elections!!," quips one post, "If you believe that, we deserve what is coming...if you don't then it is time for you to suit up ruck up and get ready for battle tomorrow #stormthecapitol." Here the act of voicing dissent is framed as too passive to enact any real change. "Gathering is great...makes you feel good," admits the same user, posting from Freedom Plaza, but "it's like political masturbation. #stormthecapitol and arrest the Seditionists? You ready for that folks?" The same sentiments can be seen in the next post, where shock at defeat quickly turns to a urgent call to take up arms: "WE JUST ESSENTIALLY GOT VOTED OUT OF OUR OWN COUNTRY YOU FUCKING MORONS!!! ... PUT DOWN YOUR FAGGY TRUMP SIGNS AND PICK UP AN AR-15!!!!! WAKE UP CHILDREN, IT'S TIME TO GO TO WAR!!!!!" Across these posts, traditional political activity is dismissed as sign-waving or feel-good congregating that accomplishes nothing. This weak activity is derided, while violence is celebrated as the only means of bringing about real change.

If violence in general is called for, lynching is one frequent and disturbing form of this call. Early analysis of the event has pointed out the similarities between this pro-Trump mob and the earlier lynch mobs operating between the 1890s and 1920s in the southern United States.[41] These calls, along with similar calls on Parler to hang "Hussein Obama," demonstrate a deeply racialized vein running through these incitements to violence. Lynching is white supremacy at work, an extralegal form of punishment that flagrantly takes justice into its own hands. At the same time, hanging has a long history as a state-sanctioned punishment for the crime of treason, a strong association that Parler users draw upon. One poster offered to "build the gallows to hang the traitors for free.

Joe Biden first." Another provides a warning to "Mitch McConnell and the other 534 assholes up there in our house" that if they do not do the right thing, they will "hang from the trees on the White House lawn." Lynching thus brings together the "white supremacist justice"[42] of the deep south with a patriotic justice for crimes against the nation.

In foregrounding race, these threats remind us that the ability to incite violence often relies heavily on whiteness. "You know whose lives DONT MATTER ??? BLM AND ANTIFA !!! NOT A FUCKING ONE IF THEM DESERVES TO BREATHE !!!!" reads one Parler post. This violent threat takes on a darkly racialized tone through its reference to breath, recalling the suffocation of George Floyd in 2020 by a group of police officers. In these contexts, whiteness provides a kind of innate protection even while openly calling for a violation of the law and the death of others. The white subject gets to frame these calls to violence as free speech, while the black or brown body must reckon with them as another layer of incrimination. "In one America, you get killed by sleeping in your car, selling cigarettes or playing in your backyard," stated one black activist, "in another America, you get to storm the Capitol and no tear gas, no massive arrests, none of that."[43] Admittedly, there have been arrests since that particular statement was made. But that process has been slow and very civil, particularly when compared with the militarized and often brutal police presence used on the Black Lives Matter movement.[44] Despite some cosmetic "justice," then, the quote above still points to a broad and troubling truth. To be white is to enjoy the incitement to violence with a far milder set of consequences.

How will this violence manifest? One post that garnered over 35,000 impressions suggests three ways that violence might play out:

> Well if it's time then let's start seeing some head rolls dammit we've been holding the line very patiently it is time to start seeing these treasonous bastard's drop at the Gallo's lined up and shot in the firing squads or wired into the chair and the hammer falls and electricity through the persons body frying them from the inside out.

Another highly popular post, with 25,000 impressions and 68 shares, urges attackers to "Hang traitors to the United States of America!

#stopthesteal #prosecutethedeepstate." While this rhetoric is extreme, it pays to also attend to the platform metrics attached to them. Post impressions and shares are not simply trivia but demonstrate the kind of granular feedback that users can attain when proposing acts of violence. Post an idea, and then wait. A failed post will sit dormant or be rapidly buried beneath the digital deluge. A successful post will rapidly see metrics tick upward, gaining likes, comments, and reposts. Social media provides an immediate feedback loop, allowing incitements to be authored, published, and iterated to find the most "successful" variation.

What role did such incitements play in the storming of the Capitol? Grand claims that violent media has a direct causal relation to violent action should be approached with extreme caution. Yet more modestly, we can observe how these kinds of posts play out violent activity, trying out different scenarios, envisioning possible attacks, and testing the public's reaction to each possibility. This "war-gaming" of violence, while taking place through digital media, is not virtual nor inconsequential. While speculative, we might draw on parallel communities for insights as to the role these incitements play. In the Incel community, for instance, fantasies of violence against women function to "heighten and crystallize" violence.[45] In the case of serial and mass murder, scholars have suggested that ruminating on these fantasies "both conditions and provides justification, in the murderers mind, to actualize their violent plans."[46] These findings stress that incitements to violence, even if (not yet) pursued, carry out significant psychological and moral work, tabling possibilities and eroding inhibitions across an audience.

In the broader context of preparatory media, these incitements preempt and even anticipate future action, suggesting potential vectors of activity without being deterministic. "There wasn't a specific time or a formal plan," noted one researcher, but rather "an idea that was fomenting and spreading and shared approvingly between users in these extremist communities."[47] In hindsight, the storming of the Capitol should have come as no surprise, for this was a dream that had already been envisioned and endorsed through the logics of social media. Incitements to violence thus carry out a triple move: dismissing traditional political means as ineffective, insisting that violence is the only solution, and laying out an array of potential scenarios in advance. These functions contribute to the broader work that operational media carries out in scaffolding future activity.

Legitimizing

Finally, operational media legitimizes. If violence is to be expected and even embraced, this violence must nevertheless be justified. In the corpus of Parler posts, legitimation seems to take three variants. First, violence is justified as a means of restoring the country and society along with it. Violence is the bloody gateway that the nation must step through to regain its former glory. One user posted a quotation from Thomas Jefferson: "The tree of liberty must be refreshed from time to time with the blood of patriots and tyrants," suggesting that these activities remain true to the original ideals of the Founding Fathers. In this vision, the in-group retains an allegiance to the true America, while the out-group are traitors who must be punished for their betrayal. "American traitors hardly realize they are about to be reduced to little more than a fine red paste," warns one post, "Weeping. Wailing. Gnashing of teeth. It's all coming—because they have begged for it. What did they think would happen when they fucked with our Republic? 'Fiat justitia ruat caelum.'" *Fiat justitia ruat caelum*—let justice be done though the heavens fall—asserts that "justice" must be carried out, regardless of how devastating the consequences will be for those who have transgressed it. Violence is the only way to recover the Republic.

Such legitimation resonates with Sara Ahmed's discussion of white nationalist victimhood, where it is not hate that unites these actors but a love for the oppressed race-nation.[48] America, as many posts on Parler assert, has been pushed to the brink of collapse by a grab bag of enemies ranging from cultural Marxists to the Deep State cabal, Black Lives Matter supporters, and Antifa activists. These far-right "myths of imperilment" legitimize violence as a form of self-defense, rendering it not only acceptable but logical.[49] In this remarkable reversal, physical and verbal attacks on others are recast as an unfortunate but unavoidable act of defense. These people are patriots, the argument goes, sacrificing themselves to save the country. Their cataclysmic deeds will usher in a national rebirth,[50] returning the national body to some imagined halcyon period of the past. Only these visceral or even violent acts will "make America great again."

Alongside national rescue, the corpus of posts legitimizes violence by framing the current context as extraordinary, as outside the bounds of the normal. Normally these participants would abide by law and order. Normally these groups maintain friendly or even cozy relations with police,[51] as "thin blue line" flags online and off-line demonstrate. Yet these are not normal circumstances. Everything has become flipped, asserts one Parler post, including law itself: "Truth called a lie. Justice turned into an abomination. Freedom turned into slavery. Good called Evil. The Law to the Lawless." The United States has entered a "state of exception,"[52] yet it is the citizens rather than the state who have triggered it based on their anger at a "stolen election" and a fear of imminent defeat. In these unprecedented times, extralegal measures are required: law-abiding citizens will need to transcend the law in the name of public good. As one post in the Parler corpus urges: "The time for good people to do bad things has come." Actions that are typically unconscionable will become unavoidable.

A final means of legitimizing these actions is through the use of religious cosmologies. This media makes extensive use of eschatological rhetoric drawn from a Judeo-Christian background. "I pray for all my Patriot friends in D.C. tomorrow. Put on the full armor of God because the day of evil has come," states one post. Another post warns that "if the Patriots do not storm the Capitol, all is lost. If all is lost, it will be full confirmation we are in The Tribulation, seal #4." Drawing on the notion of the seven seals from the book of Revelation, the poster stresses the cosmic stakes of this event, a battle between the forces of good and the forces of evil. With "Infinite Angels behind us" and an "All Mighty God Above us," in the words of one user, this army will be unstoppable. This kind of language has a long lineage in the religious right and has been more recently adopted by QAnon.

A statement from Q, reposted on Parler, seamlessly draws together the state-of-exception rationale discussed earlier with this quasi-religious legitimization. These times are extraordinary; these are the end-times.

> If America falls so does the world. If America falls darkness will soon follow...This is not about politics. This is about preserving our way of life and protecting the generations that follow. We are living in Biblical times. Children of light vs children of darkness. United against the Invisible Enemy of all humanity.

This moment is at once unprecedented and predestined. Patriots cannot let "America fall", defending it with violence if necessary. And yet they can also rest assured that their actions, even if unorthodox, have the divine blessing. They are the "children of light" waging a righteous war against the "enemy of all humanity." One phrase that frequently appears in the Parler corpus puts it simply: "God wins."

* * *

All of these posts demonstrate how digital media operationalizes hate. White nationalism is a historical vein that can be tapped into. White loss and white rage offer powerful affective currents to draw on. Indeed, the continued relevance of these forms of identity and grievance "set the stage" for Parler, creating the conditions for its existence and success. And yet they are also ambient and free-floating, waiting to be channeled into particular expressions or actions.

Operational media draws on this white heat but structures it, coalescing it into a specific event, a specific target, a specific act of violence. By connecting people together, highlighting information, and distributing posts across a community, digital media creates organization and order. It takes indistinct rage and resentment and hones them, articulating it into a more precise agenda, a purpose, a plan. It converts broad-spectrum fury into practical action in the world, whether that action takes the form of doxxing and death threats or political protest and physical violence. Hate is structured and scaffolded in particular ways by networked media.

And it is this point which makes networked media both novel and dangerous. Hate, as we've already explored, will always reside at the heart of the human experience. Bigotry based on race, culture, or creed is ancient. But digital technologies allow those antipathies to be cultivated and articulated in new ways. At their most dangerous, they transform hate from individual rants and empty threats to a concrete program, taken up by a broad collective, with clear targets and a shared goal. This is exactly what we see in the Capitol Storming, and what we can anticipate seeing more of in the future. Digital media has become deeply entangled with daily life—and this makes it indispensable for political life.

Notes

1   Haney-López, *Dog Whistle Politics*.
2   Lopez, "Actual White Supremacist."
3   Coates, *We Were Eight Years in Power*, 615.
4   King, *Where Do We Go from Here*, 72.
5   Coates, *We Were Eight Years in Power*, 645.
6   Jung, "Constituting the Us Empire-State and White Supremacy," 15.
7   Martinot, *The Machinery of Whiteness*, 41.
8   Berlet and Lyons, *Right-Wing Populism in America*, 21.
9   Berlet and Lyons, *Right-Wing Populism in America*, 964.
10 Feola, "'You Will Not Replace Us,'" 7.
11 Johnson from the Foreword to Garis, *Immigration Restriction*, vii.
12 Feola, "'You Will Not Replace Us,'" 11.
13 Finley, Gray, and Martin, "'The Souls of White Folk,'" 5.
14 Yancy, *What White Looks Like*, 26.
15 Ahmed, "A Phenomenology of Whiteness," 150.
16 Mills, *The Racial Contract*, 47.
17 Hochschild, *Strangers in Their Own Land*, 203.
18 Feola, "'You Will Not Replace Us,'" 17.
19 Schreckinger, "Amid Censorship Fears, Trump Campaign 'checking out' Alternative Social Network."

20   Culliford and Paul, "Unhappy with Twitter, Thousands of Saudis Join pro-Trump Social Network Parler."

21   Horwitz and Hagey, "Parler Makes Play for Conservatives Mad at Facebook, Twitter."

22   Horwitz and Hagey, "Parler CEO Says He Was Fired as Platform Neared Restoring Service."

23   Thiel et al., "Contours and Controversies of Parler."

24   Heilweil, "Parler, the 'Free Speech' Social Network, Explained."

25   Lima, "Cruz Joins Alternative Social Media Site Parler in Swipe at Big Tech Platforms."

26   Timberg and Stanley-Becker, "QAnon Learns to Survive — and Even Thrive — after Silicon Valley's Crackdown."

27   Sardarizadeh, "Parler 'free speech' App Tops Charts in Wake of Trump Defeat."

28   Cameron and Mehrotra, "Parler Users Breached Deep Inside U.S. Capitol Building, GPS Data Shows."

29   Paczkowski and Mac, "Amazon Is Booting Parler Off Of Its Web Hosting Service."

30   Donk_enby, "Crash Override (@donk_enby) / Twitter."

31   Booeshaghi, "Want to Mine the #Parler Data Dump? Perform Natural Language Processing (#NLP) on the Content of the Posts? I Made a Video Showing How to Do Exactly That; Cc @parlertakes: Https://T.Co/EFDm2jR4LU."

32   Conlon et al., "Confused About Theoretical Sampling,?" 3.

33   Conlon et al., "Confused About Theoretical Sampling?"

34   Bruns and Burgess, "Twitter Hashtags from Ad Hoc to Calculated Publics"; Bruns et al., "Towards a Typology of Hashtag Publics."

35   Donovan, Lewis, and Friedberg, "Parallel Ports."

36   Zhou et al., "Elites and Foreign Actors among the Alt-Right."

37   Minkenberg, *The Radical Right in Europe*, 13.

38   boyd, "Social Network Sites as Networked Publics."

39   Argentino, "QAnon and the Storm of the U.S. Capitol"; Lourens, "Mobs, Violence and Coups."

40   Apter, *The Legitimization of Violence*, 2.

41 Jett and Robinson, "The Chilling Similarities between the Pro-Trump Mob and Lynchings a Century Ago."

42 Pfeifer, *Rough Justice*, 94.

43 Johnson, "The Storming of the U.S. Capitol Is What Happens When White Supremacy Is Coddled."

44 Pita Loor, "Why a White Mob Felt They Could Storm the US Capitol without Fear."

45 Scaptura and Boyle, "Masculinity Threat, 'Incel' Traits, and Violent Fantasies Among Heterosexual Men in the United States."

46 Murray, "The Role of Sexual, Sadistic, and Misogynistic Fantasy in Mass and Serial Killing"; Murray, "The Transcendent Fantasy in Mass Killers."

47 Wamsley, "On Far-Right Websites, Plans To Storm Capitol Were Made In Plain Sight."

48 Ahmed, *Cultural Politics of Emotion*, 42.

49 Marcks and Pawelz, "From Myths of Victimhood to Fantasies of Violence."

50 Griffin, *Fascism*.

51 Castle, "'Cops and the Klan.'"

52 Schmitt, *Political Theology*.

Gab's Friendly Hate

In the snapshot, a husband and wife stand in a living room, smiling back at the camera. The man on the left is decked out in a polo shirt and baseball cap with a crucifix on the front. The woman on the right is adorned in a plain white dress. The sun is shining and the debris of a party lingers, a translucent green balloon hovering in the background. "Our daughter turns two today," states the caption, "my mom threw an amazing zoo themed party and brought these headpieces for everyone with different animals." He sports a frog headpiece, two giant eyes protruding from either side of the cap. She joins in the festivities with a rabbit headdress, complete with two bunny ears and a carrot attached. "We're tired," the caption continues, "but we are so much in love and have never been more content with the many blessings and struggles of living our lives to glorify God and raise a family together."[1]

The post above is from Gab, and the person it depicts is Gab CEO Andrew Torba and his wife. I open with this vignette precisely because of its normality, its everyday quality. This is a portrait of family and faith, of parenthood and pride. There is nothing shocking or controversial about this post. In fact, hundreds of comments below it exude a genuine warmth, congratulating the couple on their children, their hard work, and their persistence in the face of life's struggles. And yet the post is hosted on a platform that is widely considered to be a haven for racism, antisemitism, xenophobia, and extremism. Click a few times, and you can rapidly jump from mainstream conservative tropes (small government, guns, and religion) to conspiracy theories about the "plandemic," articles accusing immigrants of rape, thinly veiled death threats to democrats, and white supremacist screeds denouncing inferior races.

Gab is a "free speech social network" with a reputation for promulgating racism, sexism, extremism, and radical right ideologies. Compared to many of its predecessors, Gab is both a more modern and more approachable platform. Gab's platform centers around gab.com, but increasingly extends to a variety of products: a chat application, a web browser, and mobile applications. Founded only a few years ago, Gab has been steadily growing since, a rise fueled by the supposed "censorship" of mainstream social media. During July 2019, 1 million people visited[2] and by January 2021 the platform was adding 10,000 users per hour.[3] By early 2021, sources put the total user base at around 4 million accounts.[4]

With its rapidly rising user base, accessible presence, and tech-savvy product suite, Gab exemplifies the new face of the radical right. In the last decade, radical right cultures have strategically employed digitally-driven tools to repackage their ideologies, cultivate new organizational and social forms, attract new audiences, and extend their influence.[5] Gab in many ways is a flagship platform, a successful blueprint that other movements and communities can follow. For this reason, it is a salient research object, a way "in" that helps us to get a "common-sense grasp of the specific and general features of this renewed radical-right energy."[6]

In this chapter, I first zoom out, exploring the birth and development of Gab—why it exists and what it seeks to accomplish. By establishing alternative digital infrastructures, Gab aims to establish a "parallel society" that upholds a certain worldview and champions certain values. A society needs to last, to not simply be a fly-by-night operation. And so the key question here is one of sustainability, the tactical moves needed to ensure a durable community. To explore these strategies, I focus on one particular Gab product, Gab News, analyzing a selection of emails received over several months. I show that Gab's mix of topics, news sources, and hate vs non-hate speech is strategic. Its mix of topics create a more expansive world; its mix of sources facilitates a more believable (yet still conservative) world; and its mix of hate contributes to a more durable (but still hateful) world. Together these aspects avoid the weaknesses of previous digital platforms and establish a more accessible and stable right-wing community. Durability matters because it demonstrates resilience against "censorship," draws together like-minded communities, and slowly builds a critical mass of users. In doing so, the platform becomes a daily environment for thousands of individuals and shapes hearts and minds. Understanding how hate is made sustainable is key for any project that aims to make it unsustainable, counteracting these ideas and building more progressive forms of politics.

Genesis of Gab

To understand Gab as a community, it's helpful to first understand its origins and vision. What is Gab, where did it come from, and what does it want? Gab describes itself as "a social network that champions free speech, individual liberty, and the free flow of information online." The platform was founded as a direct response to the increased regulation of speech occurring on Facebook, YouTube, and Twitter. From around 2013 onwards, these mainstream platforms came under increased fire for allowing diverse forms of hate speech to flourish, from Islamophobia and xenophobia to racism.[7] These criticisms became particularly intense in the lead-up to the 2016 U.S. Presidential Election, where the quantity of hateful content spiked and its political stakes became apparent.[8]

Social media companies responded (albeit slowly and unevenly), hiring more staff, formalizing definitions, and tightening speech restrictions.[9] These moves led to blocks, bans, and evictions of users. For Gab Founder Andrew Torba, this was the moment he realized that "Silicon Valley censorship was real, it was happening, and it was very obviously going to continue to get much worse."[10] In Gab's eyes, content regulation, whether through human workers or automated routines, is a threat to free speech. In this view, blocking accounts and deleting content are not done to clean up platforms, but rather to support a liberal agenda and suppress alternate viewpoints. Censored content presents a hard "truth" or uncomfortable "reality" that doesn't conform to sociocultural norms.

In response, Gab was launched in invite-only beta in August 2016. From the beginning, its point of difference was the promise of (almost) unregulated speech. According to its policy, if a user's speech is "legal under U.S. law, it is allowed on our site."[11] Any viewpoint protected by the First Amendment of the U.S. Constitution is allowed on the platform. However, Gab's policy does not allow "copyright infringement, illegal pornography, malicious defamation, spam, and true threats" and this kind of content "may be moderated or result in a ban."[12] Hate speech is conspicuously absent from this list. And what exactly constitutes a "true threat" will always be highly subjective. When posts from the Pittsburgh shooter were criticized as incitements to violence, Torba countered that he didn't see a "direct threat."[13]

Gab's policies established a free speech haven at a time of increased regulation, a safe harbor for controversial figures and their followers. Indeed, throughout 2016 and 2017, Gab's growth was directly coupled to the "Great Purge" occurring on mainstream platforms. Twitter, for example, strengthened its "hateful conduct" policies, resulting in far-right notables like Richard Spencer, Paul Town, and John Rivers receiving permanent suspensions.[14] The migration of these figureheads onto Gab drew more interest and users to the platform. Alongside these purges, articles in mainstream media also contributed to the platform's rise. While a New York Times article critiqued Gab as an "unholy mess,"[15] its profile effectively functioned as free publicity, resulting in donations to its million-dollar crowd-funding campaign and thousands of users signing up to the platform. In May 2017, Gab exited private beta and was made available to the general public.

If anti-censorship is one clear motivation for the platform's creation, less addressed is Gab's claim to be a "platform for the people." In Gab's view, Google, Facebook, and Twitter, and other tech companies form a broader regime of "Big Tech hypocrisy" and "Silicon Valley tyranny." Funded by millions in venture capital and encompassing millions of users, these companies exert enormous influence, setting de-facto standards for communicating and relating online. Of course, this critique applies most obviously to their rules about what can and cannot be said online. But more implicitly, it also chafes at the broader control of data and the loss of user agency. Gab "is a message to the tech oligarchs," proclaimed Torba, "we will replace you and The People will take back control of their data and the flow of information on the internet."[16]

Since launching its core platform, Gab has released several new products that build atop it. Launched almost immediately in 2017 was Gab Pro, a paid tier that allows group creation, larger video uploads, no ads, and other features. In February 2019, the custom browser, "Dissenter" was released, allowing users to make posts on any page online. And these have been quickly followed by other add-ons like Gab News, which sources new articles from a variety of media outlets, and Gab TV, which provides a YouTube-like experience for streaming video. Together, this wide array of products, apps, and tools exemplifies the ability of radical right cultures to embrace and exploit contemporary information technologies.

Alt Tech

While Gab's origins may be political, it is also fundamentally technical. In popular discourse, technical infrastructure is often waved away. Platforms are said to be running "in the cloud"—wherever that is. The technology "just works," so users don't need to worry about its mechanisms. But digital platforms are material, not magical. To load a page, a request is sent as a packet of information along cables. To post your video, thousands of high-resolution images must be stored on a massive hard drive. And to add that friend, software running in the backend must access a database and edit particular fields. These hardware systems and server operations are hidden, tucked neatly away in the background. Yet without them, the screens and software interfaces that typically take center stage will not function. Nothing will work.

All of this points to a simple but fundamental fact: infrastructure underpins platforms. The data economy runs on an invisible substructure of data centers, power generators, cooling facilities, server arrays, and fiber optic cables. This vast array of equipment and expertise is needed to run any high-performing platform at scale. Startups recognize this fact all too well, but can often take the easy route of outsourcing it. Amazon Web Services, a subsidiary of the tech giant that has spent millions to rapidly establish a global network of data centers, is often the first choice for cloud hosting. Other options include competitors like Google Cloud or Microsoft Azure, where users can set up an account with a few clicks in minutes. These cloud services companies will not only provide managed storage, high-speed transfers, and payment services, but—crucially for digital platforms—are also able to scale up these services on demand. When a traffic spike hits or a platform enjoys a surge of growth, the infrastructure will grow with them, pulling in as much capacity and processing power as needed.

For right-wing platforms, infrastructure is far more fraught. Early on, Gab was treated like any other startup. They used Joyent, an infrastructure-as-a-service provider based in San Francisco. And their domain name (gab.com) was hosted with GoDaddy, a popular domain company that serves thousands of startups and small to medium businesses. But in October of 2018, Robert Bowers walked into the Tree of Life synagogue in Pittsburgh and opened fire, killing eleven people and wounding six more. Bowers had a highly active account on Gab and had posted a number of antisemitic statements on his profile page that had not been taken down. After the attack, Gab suspended Bowers account and promised to cooperate with the criminal investigation, but the damage to its reputation had already been done. On the very same day, GoDaddy canceled its domain name contract with Gab, effectively making it inaccessible. Joyent quickly followed suit, announcing it would terminate services in under 48 hours. Gab's homepage claimed it was being attacked and systematically no-platformed, and that it would be offline for a period of time.

Even before then, the deplatforming of Gab had been well underway. In early 2018, Apple had removed Gab's app from its AppStore, citing pornography. A revised version submitted a few months later was rejected as well, this time for violating hate speech policies. Over on the Play Store, Gab's app for Android devices received the same treatment.

Google removed the app for contravening its hate speech regulations, stating that it did not sufficiently moderate content, including content that incited violence and attacked groups of people. A year later, the same pattern was repeated. Gab launched a standalone fundraising website hosted on Amazon Web Services, only to have it taken down for violating Amazon's policy on hateful content.

But in the face of this systematic effort to take it offline, Gab has persisted. Less than a week after the Tree of Life attack, Gab was back online. They had found a new hosting provider in Sybill Systems, a shadowy outfit possibly based in Norway. And just as importantly, they had found a domain name host in the form of Epik, a company known for providing services to far-right, neo-Nazi, and extremist sites. Most recently, Gab has begun hosting some of its content and services on its own hardware. A 2021 post from Torba documented how they installed a massive 600 terabyte machine in one of their data centers. "We do not have the luxury of being hosted in the cloud by Amazon, Microsoft, or Google web services," he wrote, "we had no choice but to build our own and invest millions of dollars in time and hardware to maintain and grow our servers."[17]

This pattern repeated when it came to payments. Earning revenue through subscription models and donations is key for any platform. But after the Tree of Life attack, Gab was blocked by major payment processing services ranging from PayPal and Venmo to Square and Stripe. Gab scrambled and managed to strike a deal with Second Amendment Processing, a niche credit card processor, by early 2019.[18] However, that company soon became entangled in allegations of financial fraud, ending the contract within a few months. To keep the money rolling in, Gab pivoted to two different payment solutions at opposite poles of the tech spectrum: cryptocurrency and mail-in paper check. At the time of writing, Gab still accepts Bitcoin, checks, and e-checks, but has added a bespoke form of payment: GabPay, their own "new secure payment processing platform." Being blocked and blacklisted by major financial companies has forced Gab to establish its own payment infrastructure.

On the app front, the same tenacity could be seen. Instructions for adding the site to a phone's home screen were given as a workaround.

Third party apps like Roma and Tootle can be configured to access Gab content. And Gab is working on developing their own phone, which would allow fine-grained control over the software that can be installed. But perhaps the savviest innovation was their release of Dissenter, a custom browser released in February 2019. Dissenter allows users to comment on any article, video, or social media post, even when commenting is unavailable or intentionally disabled. In essence, the tool is a universal commenting system with a distinct political culture baked in, enabling a layer of right-leaning content across the web.[19]

So Gab has not folded like its predecessors. After each blow to its infrastructure, it has pivoted, locating allies, signing contracts, and finding workarounds. I highlight this dogged persistence not to paint the hate haven as heroic, but to point to the dangerous innovations it has gradually assembled over time. As Joan Donovan highlights, in threatening the very survival of the movement, no-platforming efforts have forced a turn to infrastructure.[20] For every technical problem, Gab has found an alternative solution—and these solutions, stitched together, begin to form a viable alternative infrastructure. Indeed, Gab can rightly be called a leader in the Alt-Tech space, laying down a blueprint for other radical right organizations in the future. "As one of the most successful and durable platforms of the Alt-Tech movement," notes Greta Jasser and her colleagues, "Gab has been at the forefront of this new digital support infrastructure for the far right."[21] While Gab's stack may not be as polished or rock-solid as tech titans, its fundamental independence offers a model for how to survive or even thrive in the face of deplatforming.

A Parallel Society

Alt-Tech wants to replace the infrastructure of the internet with alternatives that provide the same functionality but align better politically and ideologically. As Gab's work so far has suggested, every component should be swapped out, from web browsers to hosting providers and social media platforms. Torba calls this "Building Technology To Power A Parallel Christian Society" or "Laying the groundwork of infrastructure for a parallel society." In one sense, this is banal or even boring work. It means developing software and ironing out bugs, schlepping a server into a data center and installing it, or locating and emailing technology companies to find those sympathetic to your cause. But while the work of engaging with low-level internet technologies may be dull, they matter deeply. As Donovan and her co-authors note, it is the policies and terms attached to the technologies "deep in the stack," that may become the "ultimate arbiters of what content gets to stay online."[22] That content—and the features and behaviors surrounding it—provides some of the basic conditions for community. And so it is possible to trace a connection between network infrastructures and the forms of social organization built atop it.

The Alt-Tech movement recognizes this connection, recognizes, in fact, that it spells life or death for their movement. They may gradually grow a viable community, but if their infrastructure is owned and operated by someone else, it may be switched off at any time, killing the community in its tracks. To build a parallel society, you need a parallel technicity. In response, the radical right has started taking technologies, asserting autonomy and independence over them, and remaking them in their image. There are Wikipedia alternates that seek to eradicate any hint of "liberal bias," job boards for COVID deniers who have been fired, dating sites that state they are only for White Anglo Saxon Protestants (WASPs), crowdfunding platforms that offer a safe harbor for projects that aren't "politically correct," and online video sites that will gladly host material that others deem to be "fake news."

"The result of the emerging alt-tech world," as Julia Ebner notes, "is an entirely new information, communication and socialization ecosystem."[23] To be sure, there is a kind of make-shift quality to this ecosystem. Some sites lack the polish of their mainstream equivalents; others struggled to make a profit and are now defunct. And yet as one service or platform goes offline, another one emerges to take its place. So while the execution may be uneven, the overall end-goal is clear: a parallel digital universe embedded with the correct values at its core: whiteness, patriotism, nativism, religious fundamentalism, and so on. Even now, in its nascent form, we can start to see individuals shirking the mainstream media and migrating to a parallel world.

Gab in particular voices this dissent, railing against Silicon Valley elite and Big Tech as the dictators of the digital world. For those who run and use the platform, the Valley is full of progressives and atheists, feminists and communists, people who hate the family, the church, and the nation. Torba was an entrepreneur in Silicon Valley before moving to Pennsylvania to start up Gab, and so has firsthand experience of its depravity. The inhabitants of the Valley were "narcissistic, empty, and sociopathic people" he proclaimed, inhabitants of a "nihilistic hellhole of a post-truth, post-morality, and post-Christian world." These secular degenerates stand against everything he believes in, and yet, because they design and manage the world's largest platforms and tech companies, they wield inordinate power over what people can say and do. In response, he is constantly railing against the Silicon Valley elite as censors and stiflers of free speech.

In fact, for some researchers, this is the red thread that binds the disparate community on Gab together. "What unites the '#GabFam' is more a shared sense of online persecution than a singular commitment to a specific far-right ideology," notes Jasser and her co-authors, "a perceived techno-social victimhood" at the hands of Big Tech.[24] There is a broad spectrum of people on the platform, from anti-government militants to antivaxxers, conspiracists to conservatives, white supremacists to religious fundamentalists. Yet whether banned for racism, sexism, or incitements to violence, many of the users on Gab feel they have been targeted and stigmatized for their beliefs, for speaking the truth. Some users may not exactly agree with extremists or those who use racial slurs, but this is a natural byproduct of free speech. What they can all agree on is that Silicon Valley tyranny has gone too far.

This same sentiment can be heard from users across the web. The mainstream social media platforms are a "nanny state," one man stated, constantly "jumping in and correcting things for the record" in an inappropriate way.[25] He planned to shift from these mainstream platforms to alt-tech alternatives as a way of "sending a message to them to tell them to stay out of my business." Another user stated that the "oligarchs of Silicon Valley" were controlling and manipulative, constantly censoring and demonetizing the accounts of controversial figures. "They don't have your interests at heart," he claimed, "only their vision of a world under their thumb."[26] In this climate, Alt-Tech seems to offer a revolution, replicating all the core functionality of popular platforms but also offering the ultimate feature: "placing the rights and freedoms of users first."

On the issue of tech freedom, the right-wingers of Gab find themselves strangely aligned with many on the left. The Electronic Frontier Foundation, for example, even with its more libertarian bent, has long advocated for free speech and the right to criticize those in power. For the EFF, Big Tech is constantly overreaching, threatening to undermine the digital liberties that the internet was originally framed around. Similarly the Pirate Party seeks to promote free speech, net neutrality, open access to information, and other forms of digital rights. Big Tech, with its walled gardens, privatized products, and proprietary software, is a force that stands in direct opposition to many of their aims. Indeed, these views echo Evgeny Morozov who has long criticized the major technology companies and their lucrative business model of deriving income from personal data.[27] Instead, he suggests socializing digital infrastructure and developing alternative platforms that would serve the people rather than private corporations. Gab's "platform for the people" slogan picks up on this anti-Big-Tech sentiment, leveraging a desire for agency and autonomy over our digital lives that extends well beyond the radical right.

While there are certainly political and societal shifts emerging from Alt-Tech, I'm interested most of it all in the perspective of the individual. What does it feel like to inhabit this parallel world? It brings to mind the premise of *The City and The City* by science fiction author China Mieville.[28] In the novel, the two "crosshatched countries" of Beszel and Ul Qoma lie interposed on top of each other. Each state has its own slang and language, its own history and mythology, its own distinctive social and cultural life. Inhabitants of each city have learned to "unsee" the other territory, to consciously ignore the individuals and architectures that do not belong. While physically a house or business may lie directly alongside your own, cognitively and culturally it belongs to an entirely different

world. Walking through the streets, the narrator is "hemmed in by people not in my city," strangers or aliens that he shares little with.

Would this experience, this subjectivity, come close to that of the Alt-
Tech user? This is a person who inhabits an alternative world, getting
their news, social interactions, and even their daily necessities from a di-
vergent set of companies and organizations. Indeed, Gab has already established a "parallel economy" with politicians, bands, clothing brands,
furniture studios, and soap companies all advertising on the platform. In
this world, hardworking white folks are still esteemed, Christian values
are still respected, and Trump is still president. In this world, a person
feels at home, with her kind of people, and the kinds of views that she understands and accepts. There is kind of ideological comfort here, where
individuals can lean back into a familiar and shared habitus. Nothing
needs to be explained. After all, these truths are just common sense.

While views may diverge, these views adhere to an overall conceptual
"grammar" that draws on familiar tropes of tradition, patriotism, religion, and so on. True antagonism—fundamental challenges to this way
of life—is absent. To be sure, there may be a sense of anger or even outrage at what the other side is doing—indeed, individual and collective
identity may be based on pushing back against it, whether this is anti-
black, anti-feminist, anti-LGBT, anti-government, or any combination
of the above. But there is never a space for real conflict, for the kind of
sustained and awkward confrontation where users are placed face-to-
face with one of "them" and need to rationalize or perhaps even reconcile their differences. "It's become safer to retreat into our own bubbles,"
lamented Obama in his farewell speech, "whether in our neighborhoods
or college campuses or places of worship or our social media feeds, sur-
rounded by people who look like us and share the same political outlook
and never challenge our assumptions."[29] The parallel society is bracketed
off, not only technically and financially, but epistemically, allowing individuals to retain and even double down on their beliefs.

Sustainable Hate

How is this parallel society constructed and perpetuated? Here we're interested above all in the question of sustainability, in the strategic steps taken by the radical right to survive and even thrive. Creating a platform is easy. Creating a platform with controversial content, that avoids legal, technological, and political attacks, attracts a broad audience of users, and develops into a long-lasting and lively community, is much harder. Many radical right sites have sprung up with much fanfare, but failed to attract a community or funding, becoming mothballed or simply falling into oblivion. A list of these digital ghost towns would include Hatreon, WrongThink, InfoGalactic, PewTube and Voat, all platforms that are now defunct or offline. While those sites are dead in the water, Gab continues to add users, to install new servers, and to bring new sponsors onboard. Why has Gab succeeded, when so many before it have failed?

To answer this question, I zoomed in on one particular product, Gab News, a daily email newsletter with hand-picked headlines that interfaces with its broader platform. Investigating an official product goes against the grain of much Gab research, which has been heavily focused on user content. Academic studies have collected and analyzed millions of posts, aiming to quantify their level of hate,[30] investigate the prevalence of Islamophobia,[31] or trace the spread of antisemitic myths[32] on the platform. The same focus on Gab's users is seen in many journalistic accounts. News media have concentrated on individuals and their hateful comments, particularly in the case of "real world" violence. For instance, antisemitic statements on the Gab page of the Pittsburgh synagogue shooter have been widely noted.[33] Yet if connections between extremists and Gab are important, as critiques they are piecemeal and limited, allowing Gab to disown these users as fringe cases. Such individuals are anomalies, the argument goes, who posted incendiary material that was unfortunately overlooked. Their messages were removed; their account was deleted. They are outliers who do not represent the Gab platform and its typical user-base.

By contrast, the content on Gab News cannot be so easily dismissed. These are news articles that have been curated directly by Gab, hand-

picked from the thousands of possible articles that could have been chosen that day. This content is intentional, the result of a particular human decision that deemed it noteworthy. And these decisions are linked
closely to Gab itself as an organization, highlighting its ideologies and
its concrete contributions to the platform's broader culture. Rather than
isolated individuals, this focus foregrounds Gab itself as a key player in
a wider system. In essence, Gab News provides a window on the official Gab imaginary, the "authorized" version of right-wing culture propagated by the company itself, its director, and its staff.

Launched in August 2019, Gab News is essentially an email newsletter, with each email containing between 5 and 10 news headlines. Each
headline links through to a unique landing page on the Gab website,
which contains the same headline and a short description. Upon clicking
this link, users are taken to the original article. To research Gab News,
I established an email address and received Gab News emails over the
course of several months, receiving dozens of emails with hundreds of
headlines. After collecting all of this material, I analyzed it with three
different methods. The next three sections step through each analysis
and then discuss what I learned.

A More Expansive World

First, I classified articles by topic. A classification scheme was established by surveying the articles and noting recurring themes, while
also being informed by my previous work on radical right cultures and
their broader ideologies. I arrived at the following categories: Politics,
Race, Moral Decay, Media, Freedom, Immigration, Economy, and the
Environment. While most categories are self-explanatory, a few require
unpacking. Many articles were political in the sense of foregrounding
power relations, but "Politics" was strictly reserved for stories on the upcoming election, politicians, and parties. "Moral Decay" encompassed
stories deploring the decline of traditional values and the depravity
accompanying it. Articles on sexual perverts, abortion clinics, and the
erosion of the family characterize this category. Finally, the "Freedom"

category focused on threats to individual and civil liberties. Articles discussing the surveillance state, police overreach, and Big Tech were key examples here. Because of the predominance of COVID-19 during this period, I ignored any story that was purely pandemic related, but included it in other categories if it included an obvious sub-theme. This approach was rationalized because a number of COVID-19 articles contained a strong subtext. "Coronavirus Patient Zero in Italy Was Pakistani Migrant Who Refused to Self-Isolate," for instance, clearly uses the virus to push a xenophobic message.

This topical analysis gestures to a heterogeneous mix of content. Rather than focusing heavily on a single area, a variety of topics, issues, and events are discussed. Certainly there are variances here, with Politics (18%) slightly overshadowing categories like Race (15%), Moral Decay (14%) and Freedom (14%). But this content is not dominated by a single category. Articles range from government policy ("Hungary's Pro-Family Policy Working, Births Up 9%") to media monopolies ("Is Apple an Illegal Monopoly?") and the politics of gender in sports ("State gets sued for allowing only girls in girls' sports"). The key pattern is diversity, a more comprehensive media environment that encompasses a wider range of issues.

Gab's broad mixture of topics establishes a more expansive and multifaceted world. Gab has openly stated that it wants to expand its userbase, to bring in new demographics, and to create an alternative media ecosystem.[34] Its "platform for the people" slogan signals this vision. In this sense it abandons the strategy of historical "communities with closure"[35] who maintained nationalist and racist viewpoints by bracketing out the world and isolating their members. To reach this goal, it needs to go beyond single issues that are only relevant to a narrow band of society.

For this reason, we see a broad constellation of topics and themes across Gab News, with each article acting as a potential access point into the Gab community. This can be seen most clearly in the range of articles that are not about "politics" in the strict sense of parties, elections, and leaders. These are articles like "Sweden: Hijab is Look of the year," "University bans emails that 'insult' or 'embarrass' people," "Marriages among opposite-sex couples fall to a record low," or "Demand for meat rising despite deluge of plant-based alternatives." These articles touch on academia, fashion, diet, marriage, and become an entry point to people interested in these areas. It is telling that the same seemingly unfocused communication strategy is used by anti-vaxx groups, with scholars noting a "broader range of flavors" across messages that appeal to a "broader cross-section" of individuals.[36] Each piece of communication is an invitation into the community, a pathway to joining their ranks.

When this invitation is taken up, the user gradually moves into the group. The vast array of headlines, texts, imagery, and video form a "shared symbolic space"[37] on the platform. Gab users respond to this media with disbelief or fear, with affirmation or outrage. In doing so, they construct a collective understanding of the world and themselves as a group. This is how community is built—indeed this activity is one of the key requirements for community. As Cohen notes, community members believe they have "a similar sense of things either generally or with respect to specific and significant interests."[38] Communities make sense of things in the same way; their interpretation of events is shaped by a common set of desires and values.

The group provides individuals with belonging, a deep-seated need driven by our human desire for "social contact, interaction, support and affective exchange."[39] Gradually each person develops a sense of belonging—psychologically they feel connected to a group of people, proud of that group, and feel they are a valuable member of it.[40] Belonging is key for understanding the allure of Gab at a time when many are experiencing acute loneliness and its detrimental effects.[41] Indeed, researchers of adjacent right-wing communities like QAnon have noted how important this sense of community is, with many members testifying how isolated or alone they felt prior to that point.[42]

However, communities are defined not just "by what is shared, but by what is distinguished."[43] Boundaries are a vital part of community building, and the work of demarcating and policing the lines between "us" and "them" is constant. If Gab's diverse array of media draws users into a community, it also inherently establishes a highly articulated border setting them against other communities. Each article is a package of rhetoric that can form what Kenneth Burke called "cluster agons" or

"God-Devil" terms. Every issue matters to somebody and so any issue can act as a "wedge issue,"[44] a rhetorical strategy that creates factions and delineates between in and out groups. While these issues may be minor, they hold the potential for establishing a point of difference or even "intransigence"[45] with one group clearly on the right side and unwilling to compromise. In doing so, each issue contributes to the crucial work of establishing borders between the Gab community and other communities.

How does Gab's content contribute to border-building and othering? Amongst the articles on Gab News, well-known controversies like immigration and homosexuality certainly appear. These are national or even international issues, grand struggles which often pit the Republicans against the Democrats, conservatives against the progressives, or the left against the right. In this sense, these articles conform to what Karell and Freedman term "rhetorics of subversion."[46] In their study of texts produced over two decades by radical groups, the researchers noted the prevalence of this rhetorical theme, an outwardly-oriented motif focusing on enemies of the group and their ongoing war against them.

However, alongside this theme, Karell and Freedman also identified a "rhetoric of reversion" with a more inwardly-oriented focus.[47] These types of texts urged members to "change society by turning towards their immediate social and temporal context—including themselves—in an effort to exclude unwanted beliefs, behavior, people, and organizations."[48] This rhetorical theme can also be seen on Gab News, as the headlines above on sport, diet, fashion, and other ostensibly "apolitical" topics attest. These are small things, everyday issues, local or personal concerns. They suggest that the scope of the culture wars are being broadened, that a line is being drawn through a far more expansive set of issues.

Indeed, these kinds of stories pose the question of whether some of Gab's success is due to this further foray into everyday life. Adjacent right-wing communities like QAnon provide a strong example of this tactic. Scholars have noted that QAnon successfully used personal interests such as natural parenting, yoga and fitness, homecare brands, and lifestyle blogs to draw in new demographics.[49] Similarly, QAnon's conspiracy around child sex-trafficking and its cooption of the "save the children" slogan preyed on familial and maternal fears to pull in a diverse array of women.[50] More recently during the pandemic, masking—a seemingly small, individual choice about whether to cover your face with cloth—has been successfully leveraged into a major point of division, with groups using this controversy to build cohesion and mobilize financial support.[51] These examples show the power of groups who go beyond the "political" in the strict sense of the term. Paradoxically, by latching onto the "personal," they are able to build significant traction and leverage it towards significant political force.

A More Believable World

Next, I classified articles by source. For this schema, I employed a more a-priori approach to coding,[52] drawing on the well-known "Media Bias Chart" established by Ad Fontes Media to classify media outlets. Ad Fontes is a Public Benefit Corporation that uses human analysts with a broad array of political views to rate news sources.[53] For more obscure news sources that weren't included in the Media Bias Chart, I drew upon the Media Bias/Fact Check database, an independent media organization that rates over 3000 sources according to bias and reliability.[54] The Media Bias Chart uses a dual axis approach, with sources rated by "Reliability" on the y-axis and "Political Bias" on the x-axis.

First, the Political Bias dimension. By categorizing the source of each article and totaling their numbers, a portrait of Gab News sources begins to emerge. Here "conservative," "very conservative," and "extremely conservative" categories are (very roughly speaking) similar in makeup, constituting 35%, 16%, and 27% of articles respectively. To be sure, there are variations in these figures, with some categories weighted more or less in the mix. But the key point is that there is a mix, with articles sourced across a political spectrum. This becomes more obvious when the smaller liberal and neutral figures are combined into a single category, forming another 22% chunk of articles. In essence, the result is a pie with four similar sized pieces. This light analysis shows that Gab's articles are not wholly drawn from hyperconservative outlets. Certainly right-wing mainstays like Breitbart and Infowars do appear amongst the sources. But they are augmented by slightly liberal sources like the *Los Angeles Times* and essentially neutral outlets like ABC News and Al Jazeera.

The mix of Political Bias is directly linked to a mix of Reliability. According to the Media Bias chart, websites like Infowars and Summit News combine a hyperconservative political stance with false or invented claims. These outlets weave together conspiracy theories with purely fabricated stories, epitomizing an extreme form of "fake news." However, alongside such sources, Gab also pulls articles from more mainstream conservative outlets like *The Daily Mail* and the *New York Post*. In the chart, these outlets do not reach the category of propaganda but are rather classified as "opinion." Gab supplements this mixture by drawing on heavyweight outlets like the *Wall Street Journal* and the *India Times*, which Media Bias deems journalistically impartial. And at times, Gab even draws from outlets like TMZ, a left-leaning magazine with a more sensationalized approach to claims.

This mix of sources across Gab News contributes a certain legitimacy. Established mainstream sources have a reputation for factual reporting and analysis. Placed in this mix, they bring with them some of their dependability and trustworthiness. They confer authority on the broader mix of articles. Here we see a hybrid communication strategy, with Gab strategically combining left-leaning and neutral sources with conservative and hyperconservative outlets. As communication scholars have demonstrated, credibility and authority can be obtained by splicing together hyperpartisan right-wing concepts with more established mainstream news media.[55] In this sense, propaganda "borrows" believability from the reputation of the articles surrounding it.

Indeed, in Gab News emails, headlines from well-known neutral sources are often placed above or below more stridently conservative headlines. For example, Gab News from March 17 contains a link to a story from ABC News: "Global stock markets, US futures fall after Fed rate cut." This is a decidedly straightforward or even dry piece of reportage focusing on interest rates and the economy. However, directly below this is a link to a story from Summit News: "Denmark Passes Law

Enabling Forced Coronavirus Vaccinations." Summit News, as mentioned above, is considered to be an extremely conservative outlet that regularly peddles conspiracy theory and fabricated stories.

While the veracity of these sources varies enormously, visually they appear identical. Each headline is placed on equal footing; each headline seems just as valid as the one that precedes it. This ambiguous blend reflects long standing techniques of "grey propaganda," a "tricky fusion of 'true' news and factually correct content with rumor-mongering fictions" that is much more difficult to untangle and evaluate.[56] Rather than being made up purely of wild claims or "obvious" conspiracy theories, the content here is a heterogeneous mix of facts and fictions, opinions and editorials, the slanted and skewed. When users move between one source and another, there is no break or obvious disjuncture. In fact, clicking each link leads firstly to the Gab News landing page for each article rather than the originating website, further unifying their presentation and giving them similar credence. Like broadcast media, Gab News establishes credibility via a smooth "transition between objective reporting and subjective commentary."[57]

And yet if this is a mix, it is a distinctly conservative one. While Gab News weaves in roughly a quarter of liberal and neutral sources, the remaining three-quarters consists of conservative, hyper conservative, and extremely conservative media outlets. There is no sense of providing "both sides" here. The spectrum of sources, while diverse in their political affiliations, consistently skews towards the right and far-right. The mix is only balanced if one has already adopted a rather conservative worldview. As scholars have shown, these "echo chambers" or "filter bubbles" have the ability to reinforce or even intensify an individual's social and political viewpoints.[58]

This fundamental bias suggests that some of Gab's "diversity" is superficial rather than structural. It indicates an information environment that may appear varied, yet also bracket out viewpoints that seriously contradict an established worldview or narrative. What remains is a carefully delineated world of compatible ideas curated to attract like-minded individuals. As media scholar Wendy Chun reminds us, homophily "closes the world it pretends to open."[59] Digital social media platforms may feature an array of views or even promote debates while simultaneously locking out content which is truly unwanted, unexpected, or otherwise ideologically threatening. Putting this point together with the previous section gestures to the power of the Gab News blend: hybrid sources provide legitimacy, presenting a believable slice of reality, yet constantly reinforce a decidedly conservative understanding of events and issues.

A More Moderate World

Finally, I looked at the Landing Page associated with each Gab News article. In general, Gab News articles were more moderate rather than explicit in their rhetoric. Stories do tend to uphold certain norms (white, conservative, Christian, heteronormative) while devaluing others, but they do so in subtle ways, often framing issues as threats to freedom or a decay of morals. Forms of prejudice and degradation certainly still persist, but they are implied. Xenophobia, for instance, is not stated outright, but instead becomes a more ambient anxiety that hovers across a diverse array of topics: labor and jobs, borders and migration, health and the coronavirus. The shocking hate seen in legacy hate havens like the chans—racial slurs, calls for genocide, violent imagery—is nowhere to be found here. In fact, within these articles, hate speech in the strict sense does not exist at all. I compiled a subset of 40 articles and checked them against a "hate lexicon" of 187 hateful terms compiled by researchers.[60] None of these terms were found, with the exception of "queer" which was used in a neutral rather than hateful manner.

Of course, this doesn't mean that hate speech disappears from the Gab platform. Beyond the "official" Gab product of News, there are numerous posts on both group and personal pages that are overtly racist, sexist, xenophobic, or otherwise hateful. And this paradox begins to suggest a hybrid, Janus-faced form: a more private form of explicit hate that stands alongside the more tempered and public-facing media showcased by Gab News.

In fact, this is precisely what we see on each Gab News Landing Page. After clicking a headline from a Gab News email, the user is not taken directly to the original story, but to a short interim page on Gab that contains the title, a short description, and a hyperlink to the source. Directly below these summary fields is a discussion section where users running Gab's custom "Dissenter" browser can post comments on the story. It is here that hate emerges in highly explicit ways, from racist epithets to misogynistic slurs, threats of physical violence, and advocations for genocide.

For example, a story with a headline such as "New Zealand Goes Into Lockdown After Just Four New Cases of Coronavirus" clearly has a political angle, but conforms more or less to journalistic phrasing, with a thumbnail of Prime Minister Jacinda Ardern alongside the headline. Yet the Dissenter comments below range from "hang that evil tranny tyrant" to asking "how the fuck did this bitch get elected? She's not even remotely attractive" and calling Ardern a "cunt" that has embraced the "PedoElite." Another story on NBA protests, while again with a strong headline—"Trump Slams NBA Players Over Protests"—would not be out of place as an op-ed in traditional news-media. But once again, the top comment below the summary with the most upvotes—"well no shit they are garbage human beings with one capability: to throw a ball through a metal ring"—reveals how this story is interpreted by Gab readers, confirming a deeply dehumanizing and highly racist worldview.

If the "official" Gab News narrative remains relatively tempered, then, these comments disclose a more extreme and overtly hateful ideology that intersects with it. These stories seem to offer users a springboard for animosity, a diverse set of global events and issues that can be interpreted through a hyperpartisan lens. Here we see the resurgence of the "'us versus them' lens through which the Far Right usually understands the political world," a lens that "conforms to a media logic that demands the simplification of news stories and the adoption of conflictual frames."[61] The Dissenter comments demonstrate that traditional animosities such as white supremacy, xenophobic nativism, and virulent misogyny have not disappeared on Gab, but have rather been reincorporated through platform-driven capacities into a kind of internal channel. The publicly-facing media of Gab News, while undoubtedly opinionated and political, remains relatively civil and approachable, while the Dissenter comments on each story engender a backchannel for hate.

Gab's mixed hate discussed above is a communication strategy. It responds to the problem of sustaining community in an environment where hateful individuals are increasingly de-platformed, hate speech is identified and regulated, and toxic communities are shut down. Gab seems to have understood that explicit hate speech can become a weakness, a vulnerability undermining a platform's appeal and long-term prospects.

First, explicit hate speech makes content a target. Companies like Facebook now employ thousands of workers to moderate content, while automated hate speech detection has attracted countless studies.[62] Of course, these "solutions" are far from perfect. Identifying and removing hate speech, whether through human or software-based approaches, remains difficult. But the key point here is that toxic speech is a target. When hate speech is identified, images are removed, groups are flagged, and accounts are deleted. Users must battle against content moderators, uploading and re-uploading controversial posts. Such practices are hardly viable as a long-term strategy. Rather than a durable foundation for radical right cultures, content becomes unstable or even invisible.

Second, overt hate makes the community itself a target. Toxic communication draws attention to a forum or platform, providing ammunition for those who wish to see it removed. Exhibit A is 8chan. Driven by shock tactics, the virulent racism, sexism, and xenophobia on the platform were extreme and on-the-nose. Terminology, from the n-word to neologisms like "cucks" mixed racial slurs with terms of sexual humiliation. Posts called for the genocide of various races and violent terrorism against immigrants. And image memes spliced together Nazi dog whistles with thinly veiled references to rape, incest, and death. Of course, the shock of such dark "humor" was precisely the point, a gleeful mix of sadism and racism done "for the lulz."[63] Yet 8chan drew increased fire from organizations, and even its founder admitted it had the "worst content on the internet" and should be taken offline.[64] This toxic content and its concrete connections to acts of physical violence resulted in increasing calls to shut it down. In late 2019, its hosting company suspended 8chan's service, defending the takedown by describing it as a "cesspool of hate."[65] The same pattern occurred with Reddit's most notorious communities: r/CoonTown and r/fatpeoplehate. These groups were blatant in their hate of certain groups, their vicious shaming of others, and the explicit language used to do so. This reputation rendered them clear targets for takedowns. Shortly after implementing its anti-harassment policy in 2015, Reddit closed both subreddits.[66] Purely toxic communities, with no "redeeming" features, come under pressure.

Finally, and most fundamentally, explicit hate speech is limited in its appeal. It is discordant or even jarring when set against the (supposed) progress and tolerance of our contemporary moment, at least in the public sphere. "In the United States," noted one article, "declines in the overt expression of racial prejudice over several decades have given way to near universal endorsement of the principles of racial equality."[67] In this environment, even the editor of one hate haven recognized that "raging vitriol" was "a turnoff to the overwhelming majority of people."[68] Such violent language often presents a caricature of the "other," an obvious stereotype that is easy to dismiss. Extreme hate speech tends to isolate a subgroup, constraining its reach and influence on the mainstream. This "in your face" rhetorical strategy is too blatant to function persuasively.[69] It cannot achieve broad appeal and so cannot function as an adequate foundation for the future.

Together, these three factors come together to frame explicit hate speech as a vulnerability. Overt racism, sexism, and xenophobia marks its authors and their environment, exposing them to censorship and criticism on multiple fronts. From a strategic perspective, hate speech engenders fragility and instability, undermining efficacy and influence. Gab's mixed hate avoids many of these weaknesses. Official products like Gab News are more moderate in their rhetoric, showcasing articles that may be conservative or even hyperconservative but which never veer into the explicit hate (white supremacy, misogyny, and so on) seen on legacy platforms. This more tempered rhetoric is also more defensible, falling comfortably within the Overton window of publicly acceptable speech.[70]

And yet, as the previous section showed, explicit hate on Gab is only a few clicks away. Gab is able to usher in a broad demographic with its "softer" or "lighter" material but also offers an easy pathway to "harder" or more "explicit" hate. This dynamic allows individuals to be gradually indoctrinated to more extremist ideas. Instead of being confronted immediately with racism, antisemitism, and other attacks, users begin from a more moderate basis. This "soft sell" approach seems more successful because such viewpoints fall within the latitude of people's acceptance and are more likely to be incorporated into their attitude structure.[71] Once acclimated to these lighter versions of bigotry, Gab users have numerous pathways to more strident or explicit material. Such digitally-mediated pathways mirror the "alt-right pipeline,"[72] with ex-radicals testifying how they began with mainstream material but gradually progressed to channels that endorsed white supremacy, ethnonationalism, and other far-right themes. And disturbingly, this analysis aligns with insights from terrorism studies. Scholars have noted how incremental radicalization is,[73] with extreme beliefs like violence only being introduced and rationalized at the end of this pathway.

* * *

How is hate made sustainable? With its strategic mix of content and packaging, Gab provides the blueprint, showing how to avoid known vulnerabilities and build a durable community. Gab offers more expansive world, a "big tent" community spanning many a number of topics, issues, and events. It presents a more believable world, splicing together mainstream sources with marginal outlets to bolster its credibility. And it offers a more moderate world, avoiding demonization and deplatforming by toning down views (at least in its official products).

All of these aspects contribute to Gab as an accessible and inviting world, suggesting strong reasons for the platform's success and its ability to mobilize a significant community. Yet if Gab offers a diverse and generally more tempered entry point for users, it nevertheless retains an undercurrent of explicit hate where virulent racist, sexist, and xenophobic concepts are on full display. Indeed, it is this combination of accessibility and extremism that I believe makes this platform particularly potent. Gab is the friendly face of hate, a user-friendly platform open to all where a broad array of views can be defended under the mantra of "free speech"—yet users can also smoothly progress to harder or more explicit material as they become acclimated over time.

Notes

1   Torba, "My Daughter Turns Two Today."
2   Gilbert, "Here's How Big Far Right Social Network Gab Has Actually Gotten."
3   Brandt and Dean, "Gab, a Social-Networking Site Popular among the Far Right, Seems to Be Capitalising on Twitter Bans and Parler Being Forced Offline. It Says It's Gaining 10,000 New Users an Hour."
4   Lee, "Inside Gab, the Online Safe Space for Far-Right Extremists."
5   Bartlett, Birdwell, and Littler, "The New Face of Digital Populism"; Fuchs, *Digital Demagogue: Authoritarian Capitalism in the Age of Trump and Twitter*; Guynn, "'Massive Rise' in Hate Speech on Twitter during Presidential Election"; Lima et al., "Inside the Right-Leaning Echo Chambers"; Matamoros-Fernández, "Platformed Racism."
6   Thurston, "Back to Front Truths," 197.
7   Carroll and Karpf, "How Can Social Media Firms Tackle Hate Speech?"; Chetty and Alathur, "Hate Speech Review in the Context of Online Social Networks"; Goldman, "Big Tech Made the Social Media Mess. It Has to Fix It"; Matamoros-Fernández, "Platformed Racism"; Mathew et al., "Spread of Hate Speech in Online Social Media."
8   Guynn, "'Massive Rise' in Hate Speech on Twitter during Presidential Election."
9   Facebook, "Mark Zuckerberg Status Update"; Twitter, "Progress on Addressing Online Abuse."

10   Torba, "Happy 3rd Birthday, Gab.Com."
11   Gab AI, "Frequently Asked Questions."
12   Gab AI, "Frequently Asked Questions."
13   Garsd, "Free Speech Or Hate Speech."
14   Ohlheiser, "Banned from Twitter?"
15   Roose, "The Alt-Right Created a Parallel Internet. It's an Unholy Mess."
16   Torba, "Happy 3rd Birthday, Gab.Com."
17   Torba, "Building Technology To Power A Parallel Christian Society."
18   Owen, "Gab Is Back in Business after Finding a Payments Processor Willing to Work with the Alt-Right."
19   Gilbert, "Users of Far-Right Social Network Gab Can Now Comment on the Entire Internet."
20   Donovan, Lewis, and Friedberg, "Parallel Ports," 50.
21   Jasser et al., "Welcome to #GabFam."
22   Donovan, Lewis, and Friedberg, "Parallel Ports," 62.
23   Ebner, "Replatforming Unreality."
24   Jasser et al., "Welcome to #GabFam."
25   Bomey, "Parler, MeWe, Gab Gain Momentum as Conservative Social Media Alternatives in Post-Trump Age."
26   Cheah, "The Current State of Alt-Tech."
27   Morozov, "Socialize the Data Centres!"; Morozov, "After the Facebook Scandal It's Time to Base the Digital Economy on Public v Private Ownership of Data."
28   Mieville, The City & The City.
29   Obama, "President Obama's Farewell Address."
30   Zannettou et al., "What Is Gab?"
31   Woolley, Pakzad, and Monaco, "Incubating Hate: Islamophobia and Gab."
32   Kalmar, Stevens, and Worby, "Twitter, Gab, and Racism."
33   Zezima and Lowery, "Suspected Synagogue Shooter Appears to Have Railed against Jews, Refugees Online." Foley, "Pittsburgh Suspect Robert Bowers Wrote Anti-Semitic and Racist Posts on Social Media." Roose, "On Gab, an Extremist-Friendly Site, Pittsburgh Shooting Suspect Aired His Hatred in Full." McIlroy-Young

and Anderson, "From 'Welcome New Gabbers' to the Pittsburgh Synagogue Shooting."

34   Ehrenkranz, "Gab, a Haven for White Nationalists, Is Now Trying to Reach Young, Diverse Progressives."

35   Couldry, "Alternative Media and Mediated Community."

36   Sear et al., "Quantifying COVID-19 Content in the Online Health Opinion War Using Machine Learning."

37   Silverstone, *Why Study the Media?*, 98.

38   Cohen, *Symbolic Construction of Community*, 16.

39   Damasio, Henriques, and Costa, "Belonging to a Community," 128.

40   Newman, Lohman, and Newman, "Peer Group Membership and a Sense of Belonging."

41   Killgore et al., "Loneliness."

42   Bloom and Moskalenko, *Pastels and Pedophiles*.

43   Silverstone, *Why Study the Media?*, 99.

44   Wiant, "Exploiting Factional Discourse."

45   Heinkelmann-Wild et al., "Divided They Fail."

46   Karell and Freedman, "Rhetorics of Radicalism."

47   Karell and Freedman, "Rhetorics of Radicalism."

48   Karell and Freedman, "Rhetorics of Radicalism," 27.

49   Argentino, "Pastel QAnon."

50   Bloom and Moskalenko, *Pastels and Pedophiles*.

51   Glennon, "The Anti-Mask Movement and the Rise of the Right in Ireland"; Knapton, "Rise of the Anti-Maskers."

52   Saldaña, *The Coding Manual for Qualitative Researchers*.

53   Ad Fontes Media, "Ad Fontes Media."

54   Media Bias Fact Check, "Media Bias/Fact Check—Search and Learn the Bias of News Media."

55   Farkas and Neumayer, "Mimicking News."

56   Piette, "Muriel Spark and Fake News," 1581.

57   Landreville and Niles, "'And That's a Fact!'"

58   Ingrams, "Connective Action and the Echo Chamber of Ideology"; Kashima et al., "Ideology, Communication and Polarization"; Pariser, *The Filter Bubble*.

59   Chun, "Queerying Homophily," 60.

60   Mathew et al., "Spread of Hate Speech in Online Social Media."
61   Ellinas, *The Media and the Far Right in Western Europe*, 34.
62   Djuric et al., "Hate Speech Detection with Comment Embeddings"; Fortuna and Nunes, "A Survey on Automatic Detection of Hate Speech in Text"; Zhang and Luo, "Hate Speech Detection."
63   May and Feldman, "Understanding the Alt-Right."
64   Occeñola, "8chan Is 'a Cesspool,' 'worst Content on the Internet,' Says Site Founder."
65   Prince, "Terminating Service for 8Chan."
66   Chandrasekharan et al., "You Can't Stay Here."
67   Pearson, Dovidio, and Gaertner, "The Nature of Contemporary Prejudice," 314.
68   Anglin, "Writing Guide."
69   Borgeson and Valeri, "Faces of Hate."
70   Lehman, "An Introduction to the Overton Window of Political Possibility."
71   Borgeson and Valeri, "Faces of Hate," 105.
72   Munn, "Alt-Right Pipeline."
73   Dalgaard-Nielsen, "Violent Radicalization in Europe"; Manea, "Defining the Phenomenon of Jihadist Radicalisation."

Drawn out of Hate

Last year I received an unexpected email in my inbox. "I've been looking at a lot of stuff about how people get sucked into damaging ideologies online, because my brother is a victim of this," it said. "He's a classic case," the writer continued, "isolated due to difficulty making friends, prolonged 'edgy humor' phase that became more and more unironic, consuming lots of 'anti-SJW' content like Sargon of Akkad, Jordan Peterson, etc etc. Because he's absorbed these toxic values, it now makes him almost impossible to interact with regular people."

The woman who emailed had seen one of my articles and wondered if I had any input on what could be done to reverse the process. Searching online had yielded very little that seemed relevant to her case. And the few methods she had tried hadn't seemed to make any difference. In our email exchange, there was both a palpable sense of indignation at the person her brother had become and frustration at her own inability to alter the situation. Her diagnosis of what was needed was actually highly astute, moving beyond individual ideologies to think about him as a person and the problems that drove him to this point: "social isolation, emotional intelligence, [a lack of] healthy in-person relationships." But she also recognized how difficult this process would be, refusing to don rose-tinted glasses. As she admitted in her second email: "Sometimes it looks like a hopeless case."

In this final chapter, I explore ways to draw individuals away from digital hate. As the email above suggested, this is a complex topic that is deeply intertwined with a person's background, their sense of identity, and their social environment. For this reason, there will be no grand answers delivered across these pages, no "silver bullet" solutions. My contribution will be more modest. I start by noting some issues with current counter-radicalization approaches and suggest a more holistic framing of recovery. Recovery begins with deeply understanding a person's grievances and the way that particular ideologies and communities addressed them. This is the logic of hate that the book has focused on. Logics emerge from particular environments, and so the next two sections explain echo chambers and how individuals have escaped them. I conclude by focusing once again on the whole person. Individuals are not brains in boxes with incorrect ideas, but instead unique people who need support to flourish once more, reconnecting with themselves, others, and the world.

Counter-Radicalization or Something Else?

When we talk about drawing individuals out of hate, we immediately jump to terms like deradicalization or counter-radicalization. Yet such terms are constructed in the arenas of parliaments and the corridors of state agencies. For this reason, they are tightly entangled with the spheres of terrorism, violent extremism, and national security. This is a very particular provenance, and it produces a particular framing about the threat radical ideologies create—and more problematically, the kinds of people susceptible to such ideologies. Based on this assumption, it targets particular populations with programs and educational initiatives, trying to inoculate them against the contagious influence of extremist views. Or at least this is the idea.

Deradicalization and counter-radicalization don't work, flatly asserts Tom Pettinger in a takedown article that manages to be both ferocious and meticulous.[1] While an entire industry has developed around these initiatives, their efficacy cannot be substantiated. Key terms and concepts are shrouded in confusion. Programs take place in very different contexts and employ very different methods, but are all lumped under the same heading. Closely scrutinizing key statistics like recidivism in "successful" programs reveals many to be suspiciously low or simply misreported. And the evaluation of these programs, when it does occur, is both wildly diverse and often deeply subjective.

Not only are these programs ineffective, Pettinger argues, but they actually do more harm than good. He notes that these interventions overwhelmingly target Muslim communities, despite the fact that right-wing extremism has—and continues to remain—a key issue across a number of countries. Extremism, he notes, is "almost completely" equated with Islam. It is not surprising, then, that Muslim communities feel targeted, picked out as a "suspect population" and Othered. All of this, Pettinger suggests, creates high levels of suspicion and division, ironically fostering the very kinds of conditions that governments are striving to defuse.

These latter points raise an issue in counter-radicalization that is often hiding in plain sight: race. Why is it that Islamic communities are isolated from the general population, subjected to enormous levels of surveillance and scrutiny, and enrolled in re-education programs, while white communities are largely ignored? Racial profiling and racialized decision-making are clearly at work here. Yet when we look at the discourse swirling around counter-radicalization, race is barely mentioned. Koehler's landmark study, excellent though it is, mentions race twice across three hundred dense pages.[2] In fact, in policy briefings and security reports, we tend to see a systematic attempt to avoid the term. Apart from a few rather formulaic condemnations of white supremacy, there is no serious engagement with race, with race studies, or with the deeper concept of whiteness that, as we saw in earlier chapters, was central to a number of hate formations.

The result is a kind of racial double standard that is never acknowledged. On the one hand, as Pettinger stressed, counter-radicalization places enormous pressure on black and brown communities who are already marginalized, othered, and oppressed, sowing the seeds of discord and laying the groundwork for radicalization. On the other hand, it ignores equally insidious forms of hate and bigotry that take root in white populations, dismissing these ideas and ideologies with a wave of the hand. This double standard has concrete effects, as the chapter on Parler showed. How else was it that a mob of largely white folks, many of them armed, were able to congregate in front of the Capitol, storm it, and then breezily walk out again?

If efficacy and race are issues, so are the assumptions embedded in counter-radicalization. Counter-radicalization is haunted by the possibility of a spectacularly violent act—a bombing, a shooting, an attack—and seeks to prevent this horror from happening to its citizens. To do this, it essentially rewinds time, searching for the markers and clues that might lead up to that point. In a very tangible sense, this is about pre-crime.[3] This is why we see an obsession with identifying a definitive terrorist pathway. Agencies and organizations invest enormous resources hoping to pinpoint the stepping stones that move individuals closer to that fateful moment. Whether such a pathway can be found is doubtful. Violent extremism takes so many forms, and draws on so many motivations, that a universal route seems unlikely. Regardless of whether this Holy Grail exists, the larger point here is that counter-radicalization is framed around an extremist individual and a shocking act.

But when we look at many of the stories throughout this book, we see that this moment never arrives. Individuals are certainly drawn towards hateful ideologies and hateful communities. They may harbor resentment against other religious or political groups, propagate racist and sexist material through social media, or even lash out against marginalized communities online or in-person. These animosities and attacks matter. They invoke fear and suspicion, ripping apart social cohesion and enacting a very concrete cost on their targets. And yet they never rise to the kind of violent public act that government anxieties center around.

Within their formal frameworks, would these people even qualify as radicals, extremists, or threats? Hate carries a human fallout—and digital technologies provide new ways for that hate to circulate and intensify in the hearts and minds of individuals. But this hate is also more ambient, decoupled from known terror networks or registered hate organizations. What's more, this hate sits on a broad spectrum, often not ascending to the threshold of overt violence that seems to be required. Within conventional frameworks (counter-terrorism, countering violent extremism, counter-radicalization) there is no obvious place for this more diffuse hate to sit. It goes unregistered—and this is a reason to rethink some of the terms and tools we use.

Instead of deradicalization or counter-radicalization, I suggest the word "recovery." Recovery is a more productive word in a number of senses. First, recovery does not hinge around some act of shocking violence. It is not obsessed with defusing the individual. That act, as we saw above, may never arrive. Yet that shouldn't exclude an individual from recovery and the support networks that might facilitate it. In fact, even though violence has never occurred, recovery might be something very much desired by the individual, as we'll see in the stories in this chapter.

This brings us to the second benefit of recovery: it is self-initiated. Recovery is not about coercion from above, a compulsory set of exercises rammed down the throat of the target. Instead, recovery is self-led. The individual must come to a certain inflection point and want to turn back, to somehow recuperate a life or a sense of self they feel they have lost. That journey may certainly be aided by others, as we'll see, but it must be desired and driven by the individual.

And third, recovery reinstates a degree of humanity into this concept. It steps away from the security and military jargon that pervades this space. It asserts that those caught up in forms of hate are not just threats in the abstract, a bomb in the shape of a body. They are not merely marks or targets, nameless subjects with dangerous connections and threatening ideas swirling in their head, but first and foremost, people. This acknowledgement wrests the framing away from the state and military apparatus, with their single-minded framing of threat, and opens the concept out to more holistic understandings of wellbeing. Hate is not just a weaponized agent, but a human inhibited from developing into their full potential.

The Logic of Hate

Recovery starts with engagement and empathy. To understand how to draw someone away from hate, we first need to understand what drew them towards it. This is the simple but fundamental point that drove this book. And yet, over and over again, it seems to be overlooked. Hate is a controversial subject, a charged topic that often tends to curtail any nuanced debate. Hate is evil, we are told, a set of toxic beliefs held by toxic people—and this should be obvious to all. Of course, this is not to defend hate. Racist and sexist attacks incur real human fallout. Views and actions which are anti-black, anti-immigrant, antisemitic, anti-queer, and so on should certainly not be celebrated. Yet denouncement of these powerful ideas is too quick, too breezy. When it comes to interventions, programs, and policy, the default gestures seem to be an all-too-easy condemnation followed by an impulsive shoving away. Hate is bad; and bad things must be banished.

The problem with knee-jerk dismissal is that it prevents any deeper engagement. Clearly these ideas have found significant traction across broad swathes of the population, particularly in recent years. There is something here that people find compelling and reassuring. These ideas tap into deep fears and desires; they fulfill fundamental needs. Merely denouncing them does nothing to inhibit their appeal. In fact, attaining the status of being "politically incorrect," a truth that has been censored, may only add to their allure. Philosopher Quassim Cassam makes this same point in his critique of one particular counter-radicalization initiative. "There is much talk in Prevent about the need to challenge extremist ideologies but no explanation of what makes them attractive to some people in the first place" he writes. One of the program's key myths is that "extremist ideologies can be challenged without any serious engagement with their substance or with the grievances to which they give expression."[4]

What does serious engagement look like? It does not mean condoning racism and xenophobia or defending individuals who oppress marginal groups. But it may mean temporarily deferring judgment while a set of ideas is understood and unpacked. This approach has been referred to as "methodological empathy;"[5] It begins by assuming that these ideas are not just a smokescreen, a thin distraction used by inherently hateful people to rationalize their bigoted tendencies. Instead, they are a set of "deeply held beliefs and emotionally and mythically powerful ideals about what is wrong with society and what should be done to regenerate it."[6] The aim is to get inside these beliefs and ideals, to take them apart and understand what makes them tick. In contrast to the hands-off dismissal typically taken, this hands-on approach is inherently dirtier. The researcher wades into an online mire of racial slurs, xenophobic articles, and misogynistic memes. The danger of being "poisoned by irony" and influenced by this constant deluge of material, even in subtle ways, is very real. Peers share their tips to combat this subliminal shaping, from supporting anti-hate activism to mental breaks such as taking a walk or chatting with friends.

But while this process is certainly more fraught, it can also provide deep insights into what I refer to as the logic of hate. Hate is not arbitrary or random; it does not suddenly compel a person to attack another or avoid them in disgust. No, hate is more akin to a procedure, a process that develops over time in the life of an individual. It builds atop previous learnings in a stepwise fashion, becoming more intense, more articulated, more difficult to dislodge. "Even though the media will label me a mad killer," notes the shooter in Denis Villeneuve's film *Polytechnique*, based on true events, "I consider myself a rational individual who has been pushed to take extreme measures." While outsiders may (rightly) see something pathologic, misguided, or even deranged, all of these ideas and ideologies have a degree of internal coherence, setting out a problem and "solving" it using their own terms and arguments. In this sense, every form of hate presents itself as a kind of algorithm for explaining the world: IF x AND y THEN z. By understanding these ideas on their own terms, we understand the way their core calculus operates, gaining insight into how it might be interrupted or rerouted. This is precisely what this book has aimed to do.

Understanding paves the way for intervention. A deep grasp of these ideas and the grievances they tap into (whether real or imagined) allows us to understand the story they tell. Making sense of this story allows us to tell alternate stories, or what scholars call counternarratives. Counter-narratives, as Cassam notes, carry out two tasks.[7] First, they seek to undermine the original narrative that individuals have embraced. They poke holes in its logic, they contest its claims, they point out flaws in its assumptions. All these strategies aim to unravel its promises and cast doubt on its vision. But debunking and deflating, by themselves, are insufficient. Counter-narratives must also operate positively, constructing their own compelling vision of the way the world should work. In some significant way, its version must be more coherent, more enticing, more cognitively, socially, and emotionally satisfying. In short, it must tell a better story.

What are the components of a better story, the key ingredients that might give them traction and power? Cassam suggests five elements that any compelling counter-narrative would need to provide.[8] First, Resonance: effective narratives resonate with their listeners, speaking to the lived reality of their audience. Second, Credibility: counter-narratives ring true, but also come from credible sources, people who are respected and seen as impartial. Third, Narrative Depth: stories must avoid over-simplifying and instead acknowledge complexity, history, and nuance. Fourth, Relevance: a counter-narrative must seriously acknowledge and engage with the grievances—even if misplaced—that motivate individuals. Fifth, Accessibility: at a basic level, the story must be accessible to the audience; in the context of online communities, this may also stretch into issues of tone, medium, "packaging" of the story, and so on.

All of these elements rely on a deep understanding of online communities, the cultures and practices that shape them, and the ideologies that circulate within them. These sociotechnical formations come together to weave a compelling tale about how the world works and who is to blame, one that taps directly into the grievances and fears of individuals. Only by unpacking this narrative—and the way it fulfills psychological, emotional, and social needs—can we begin to intervene within this space and suggest alternatives that might resonate with those affected. In other words, to tell a counter-story, we need to first understand the original story. And this makes the logic of hate a key foundation for recovery.

Leaving the Echo Chamber

The logic of hate emerges from a particular environment. Any discussion about "drawing out" needs to have a deep grasp of what individuals are "caught within." When looking across this book, it is clear that followers of QAnon or advocates of Gab are not merely "using" some technology, as one might use a hammer for a moment and then put it down, but rather inhabiting a world. These inhabitants are invested in this world, they feel part of the community, they are tied into a group. For this reason, it possesses a psychological or emotional hold on them, a kind of affective grip. How might we conceptualize this environment?

To answer this question, we can turn to a powerful article by philosopher C. Thi Nguyen. In recent years, terms like "filter bubble" have arisen to talk about the biases in information environments like social media. But for Nguyen, this confuses two very different phenomena. He begins, then, by suggesting two terms rather than one: epistemic bubbles and echo chambers.

Epistemic bubbles are social structures in which "other relevant voices have been left out, perhaps accidentally."[9] A Facebook feed, for example, reflects an individual's friends, preferences, and interests. It might be dominated by conservative tropes like faith and family, while leaving out progressive views related to same-sex marriage or social justice. In this sense, a personalized feed inherently creates an information environment that is partial. For Nguyen, this epistemic bubble is a "social epistemic structure that has inadequate coverage through a process of exclusion by omission."[10] Inadequate coverage, of course, matters. This blinkered information environment produces a blinkered understanding of the world, a consequence with political, social, and cultural fallout. But this selective exposure is incidental rather than malicious. For example, algorithmic filtering is one widely used mechanism that produces epistemic bubbles, curating feeds to include items that should attract attention and engagement while excluding the rest. In this case, the solution is straightforward (even if it runs against the business models of many companies): diversify the news and views that a user is exposed to. "Epistemic bubbles are relatively fragile," suggests

Nguyen, "It is possible to pop an epistemic bubble by exposing a member to relevant information or arguments that they have missed."[11]

Echo chambers, by contrast, are much more robust. For Nguyen, an echo chamber is an "epistemic community which creates a significant disparity in trust between members and non-member."[12] This is not just a matter of selectively including or excluding some information, but a more fundamental issue of defining who is trusted. The voices of members are amplified and embraced, receiving high levels of trust. The voices of non-members are distrusted through a process Nguyen calls "epistemic discrediting."[13] To see this trust/distrust binary in action, we only need to turn back to a community like QAnon. In that chapter, I showed how Q was believed to be an insider who was bestowing special or privileged information on followers. Even when predictions failed to come true, followers would claim that it was a false flag or that they had misconstrued Q's words. By contrast, those outside the community were blind to the truth. The masses are "sheeple"; government agencies are part of the deep state; pharmaceutical companies are dishonest; the mainstream media are all liars.

Discrediting is key because it creates what Nguyen calls an "epistemic buffer" that actively shields community members from contrary opinions. Even if different kinds of information somehow found their way into this environment, it wouldn't matter, because this new evidence comes from outside sources that cannot be trusted. In fact, in a perverse way, group members can anticipate contrary voices from outside and leverage them. For those on Parler, criticism of the nation and its white heritage only reinforces the fact that the country is being overtaken by progressives and cultural Marxists. For QAnoners, denial of child sex trafficking only reinforces the fact that the deep state controls mainstream media. "Of course they would say that," is the response. Contrary opinion is pre-empted and defused before it even has a chance to change hearts and minds. Through this constant process of "systematic discrediting of outsiders" and elevation of insiders, echo chambers can create "runaway credence levels for approved individuals."[14]

These reinforcement mechanisms mean that extracting someone from a hateful digital space is never just a matter of introducing new information sources or correcting some technical bias, but is always a deeper matter of trust. As family and friends of radicals have stressed, debunking facts and correcting disinformation is a losing battle. Every time a claim is contradicted, a new one rises in its place. Radicals are dug in, bunkered against voices from the outside, no matter how "reasonable" or meticulously argued. In fact, the human stories throughout this book suggest that hate's grip is deeply emotional and psychological rather than rational. For Nguyen as well, drawing someone out of these spaces is inherently a social process. "They must begin afresh *socially*," he stresses, "by re-considering all testimonial sources with presumptive equanimity, without deploying their previous credentialing beliefs."[15] In other words, moving away from hate starts by flattening the social hierarchy that has been built up. Insiders can no longer be held up as heroes or prophets; outsiders should no longer be dismissed as liars or parasites. Trust levels for all must be zeroed out.

For some, this means coming back to those who actually know them and care about them. "I miss our long/In depth talks and how you always knew what to say," wrote one Q follower to his estranged spouse, "Not what I wanted to hear but what I needed to hear. How I could get an outside perspective of the situation at hand."[16] For those caught up in hate, their closest outsider is often friends and family. These loved ones may have already tried reasoning with the follower, arguing against them, or presenting alternate viewpoints, to no avail. But as support groups suggest, patience and empathy are absolutely key and must be maintained. In testimony after testimony, ex-radicals have stressed that a starting point for recovery was finding a space or a person they could talk to without fear of being judged. "Don't give up just yet and walk away," stressed a wife who had finally had some success with her husband, "please remember there is a human being inside there who may just need a willing person to listen to them and not judge."[17] Channers know that the world regards them as disgusting, dysfunctional people. Gabbers are well aware that their values (white, Christian, heteronormative) render them regressive in the eyes of some. What they're looking for, instead, is openness and empathy. Of course, this doesn't mean that abhorrent viewpoints need to be accepted. But as we've seen repeatedly in these pages, adherence to one particular idea (in a detached, cognitive sense) was never the whole point anyway. Ideologies were always fused with broader social structures, velcroed into a broader scaffolding of connection, belonging, and meaning. "Since echo chambers work by building distrust towards outside members," concludes Nguyen, puncturing them means "cultivating trust between echo chamber members and outsiders."[18] Staying open and retaining the relationship is vital.

From Digital Detox to Digital Therapy

For some, leaving the echo chamber means leaving the bedroom, the living room, or whatever chamber they spend time online in. It entails getting off the gaming chair, shutting down the phone, and stepping outside. "I became totally fed-up with the sedentary, isolated lifestyle I had been living," stated one ex-radical, "and began to get out of the house, do things, see the world, 'touch grass' if you will."[19] The world itself can function as a kind of epistemic mirror: claims made in the funhouse of the internet can often start to look strange when held up to reality. People are not all manipulative and cynical. Out-group members are not plotting your destruction. The nation has not descended into some hellish dystopia. Such views turn out to be distorted caricatures. Once the claim is doubted, the claimer is also doubted, eroding confidence in people formerly seen as figureheads or trusted members of the community. Their fall in the minds of ex-radicals can be swift and decisive. With this growing realization, then, comes digital action: unfollowing accounts, deleting chat apps, and removing forum profiles. "As I began to see the world, talk to people, and discovered the heavy bias in the sources in which I had previously viewed the world, my extremist beliefs...began to fade away."[20]

And yet hate reversal is not simply a matter of digital disconnection. In fact, for many ex-radicals, digital spaces have been absolutely formative for recovery. As his once-impervious worldview began crumbling, one follower "began to consume material from online communities that saw through the holes in the ideas I used to hold, namely reddit posts like this one and youtube videos coming from more moderate or left-wing YouTubers."[21] As the quote alludes, a number of ex-radicals have credited so-called BreadTube or LeftTube with helping them in their journey. This loose network of content creators and vloggers creates media from an explicitly socialist, anarchist, or left-leaning perspective. But what makes this collective interesting is that they often do so by directly taking up radical right talking points and phrases. Marked up with these hashtags and labels, this media can often appear high up in search results for popular extremist tropes. In this sense, they conduct a form of "algorithmic hijacking."[22]

This is a form of technical sabotage but also an epistemic one in crossing over into a highly conservative terrain and disrupting a particular strain of thought. Indeed, empathy appears here once more as a key element. Rather than writing off right-wing narratives, these media creators work hard to understand their core logic and their powerful allure. They take up hot-button topics like cancel culture, climate change, and immigration, and treat them seriously, engaging them on their own terms. Empathetic treatment also extends to their discourse and presentation. Rather than confrontational, their presentation strategy might best be described as tangential, using satire and drama to gently poke and prod at these ideas. Creators take on alternative personas, stage wacky gags, and pile on film effects. This entertaining and almost theatrical approach moves away from the binary tactics that usually dominate this space: dry facts and scientific articles or in-your-face aggression and vitriol.

One standout example here is ContraPoints, the YouTube channel of Natalie Wynn. Her carefully constructed videos, ranging from half an hour to over an hour, home in on topics like incels, men, cancel-culture, and gender. Wynn raises the video essay to an art form, creating ornate sets brimming with props and images. She creates a whole cast of alternate personas by donning wigs, tiaras, and jewelry, carefully applying body paint, and wearing elaborate costumes. There is a sophisticated aesthetic here, but also a deliberately playful and stylish one. Lounging in a bubble bath and sipping champagne, Wynn is having fun—and fun is disarming. As one ex-radical stated: "It started off as hate watching and then it became, you know, 'Mmm, I don't hate her. She's funny.' And once you get rid of that hate you can start to actually listen to what she's saying...I couldn't tell you what it is about them, but you do not feel like you are being attacked. That's when I started to deradicalize."[23] In her video essays, Wynn directly takes up key talking points and phrases from the radical right. Rather than simply dismissing these as racist or ignorant, she unpacks each concept. Logic is certainly one aspect of this process, with Wynn exposing some of the obvious contradictions in radical right narratives. But there is always a stress on what lies at the heart of each concept: the hopes and fears that drive it. "From a psychological standpoint, you have to empathetically enter a person's world," Wynn has previously stated in an interview, "not just why do they think what they think but why do they feel what they feel?"[24]

Empathy is also a core aspect of online communities for recovery. The guidelines for ReQovery, a QAnon group on Reddit, stress that this community is not about debate but rather a place for believers to "tell their stories, receive support and share strategies and healthy coping mechanisms." The same kind of approach is used in QAnon Casualties, a sister forum on Reddit. "The most important thing to do with any Q family member or Q friend," one long-time moderator for the group stated, "is to be there for them."[25] When predictions fail to materialize and their beliefs start crumbling, they won't turn to those who gleefully dunked on them, but those who were empathetic. "You can be the bridge back to sanity," stated the same moderator.[26] Ultimately, he stressed, deradicalization is something that the follower or community member needs to do for themselves. It has to be their decision and the process has to be driven by them. And yet "having someone with them on that journey is so important."[27] While some may cynically interpret such statements as empty platitudes, they actually come from a place of deep experience. Both recovery groups have seen significant success in drawing individuals away from extremist views and toxic communities, with ex-radicals and family members thanking them for their contribution.

Funneling and Broadening

Echo chambers are often considered to be an informational or epistemic problem—and as we've seen, they certainly shape what claims can be made, who can be trusted, and what should be believed. But I'm also interested in going beyond truth-claims to consider their broader impact on the individual. In the chapter on Q, we saw how friends and family witnessed a profound change in their loved ones, a transformation so stark that they seemed to have passed away and been replaced by another person. How has this digital environment altered the self, the inner-life of the individual with their particular thoughts, hopes, dreams, and desires?

Looking back on the case studies in this book, we can see that digital technologies created an environment that narrowed and intensified certain facets of the self. In the case of 8chan, this often meant severing ties with friends, isolating oneself inside, and choosing instead to spend countless hours engaging with a playfully toxic community. In a few of these cases, traditional ideologies seemed to offer a pathway to significance, leading to an intense focus on a life-or-death issue such as the Great Replacement. As other interests dropped away, certain individuals gradually developed a high commitment to this ideology and the use of violence to achieve it, a combination that culminated in mass-murder.

In the case of QAnon, there is a similar type of funneling and filtering effect that can be seen. As their interest in Q and deep state conspiracy grows, other interests fade away, dismissed as a lie or propaganda. Friends and family who refuse to believe are seen as evil and shunned. Neophytes begin to pour more and more time into conducting their own research, watching videos, stitching together clues, and developing original theories.

The same pattern can even be found on Gab. Gabbers dismiss the mainstream media and Big Tech, retreating from the "censorship" and progressivism they see reflected in its headlines and digital spaces. In joining Gab, they exit one world and enter another, a "parallel society" that comfortably conforms to a narrow range of accepted values: white, Christian, heterosexual, and so on. In fact, part of Gab's danger, as that chapter suggested, is masking this homogeneity, providing the appearance of diversity while carefully bracketing out any significantly challenging material.

In all of these cases, we see a type of honing or tapering, where a broad array of dreams, hobbies, concerns, and social relations are stripped away and a single cause or community comes to predominate. This is not to suggest that prior to this point these individuals were ideal or altogether well-rounded. Many of the stories we have seen are marked by some kind of crisis and a sense of failure of loss. And yet, despite these issues, the same stories also gesture to family, friends, and workmates, to some outside interests or hobbies, to occasional moments of care and generosity, and to the possibility for surprising and challenging encounters—in short, to the same kind of messy, jumbled existence that characterizes the human experience. In their journey towards digital hate, these aspects of their life gradually grew fainter until they eventually disappeared altogether. Their other interests were jettisoned; their social circle constricted; their close relationships became strained. For those caught in this allure, it might be considered a kind of "purification," where things that are seen as insignificant and irrelevant are let go of. But for those around them, it seems clear what this transformation really is: a form of psychological, emotional, and relational impoverishment.

This honing of the self is about compatibility. Social psychologist Arie Kruglanski and his co-authors state that radicalization comes with a "reduced commitment to alternative, incompatible pursuits."[28] The individual identifies aspects of their identity, their relationships, and their lifestyle that either conflict with their new self or now seem obsolete. These components of the old self do not operate smoothly with the components of the new self. Friends from different races or political persuasions, partners who refuse to see the "truth," even simple encounters in the outside world—these things are errors that prevent the upgrading and remaking of the self. And so, one by one, they are deleted, creating an emptier but more compatible identity, a "streamlined self" allowing for uptake and uninhibited performance.

If radicalization engenders a funneling or narrowing of the self, then recovery should seek to undo this process. To broaden the individual, to connect them once again with things outside themselves, to open them up and out—these goals should be key. In the same study mentioned above, Kruglanski and his co-authors looked at ex-radicals, those who were drawn away from hate, violence, and extremist ideologies. As these individuals reached a turning point and started to withdraw, their words and testimonies indicated a "resurgence of alternative pursuits and objectives," or in other words, a "resurfacing of alternative concerns (e.g. for psychological comfort and tranquility) that were suppressed."[29] In some cases, people from their study became disillusioned with a religion or movement, seeing a disconnect between its high-minded ideals and the reality. In other cases, they still believed in the cause, but were no longer convinced that violence or extreme measures would further it. But in both cases, it is exposure to the messy world itself—its contradictions and contingencies—which works to undermine the thin understanding of life that once seemed so rock-solid.

In this sense, drawing an individual away from hate is less about "correcting" a particular ideology or belief, and more about staging encounters that lead someone back to a more expansive life. This insight is welcome, because it goes far beyond propaganda or re-education. It removes the tinge of moralism and self-righteousness that can creep into these kinds of discussions: you thought the wrong thoughts and believed the wrong things, now let us set you straight.[30] Instead, we can see how hate produces a constrained life, a thin and mono-dimensional existence that brackets out much of its interesting, confusing, and surprising elements as "incompatible." In the end, hate is comforting but boring. It reduces living breathing people to simple stereotypes. It flattens complex interactions into a zero-sum game. And it shrinks the verdant world into politics, narrowly understood. If this is the case, then moving away from hate is no longer a matter of thought policing, but instead of enriching a life by sprinkling social, emotional, and cultural elements back in. To be sure, these elements are not all pain-free. They also mean accepting "the ineluctable limitations and imperfections of human existence, such as transience, dissent, conflict, fallibility."[31] And yet if some of these elements bring with them intimacy and vulnerability, they ultimately result in a richer and more holistic life.

Notes

1   Pettinger, "De-Radicalization and Counter-Radicalization."

2   Koehler, *Understanding Deradicalization*.

3   Daniel Koehler, widely regarded as an expert in this space, states that "methods designed to counter or intervene in that area are automatically reaching into the grey zone of pre-criminal space. Owing to different political cultures and legal definitions, the question whether it is morally and legally legitimate to attempt to change a person's political and religious beliefs (or ideology) is consequently very controversial internationally. Nevertheless, many actors involved recognize that there is usually a highly problematic path on the radicalization process be re an individual or group acts illegally. Hence, retrospectively looking back after a terrorist attack, the radicalization processes that occur, due to a certain 'radical' ideology leading up to it, seem to justify practical approaches to avert such pathways." Koehler, *Understanding Deradicalization*, 3.

4   Cassam, *Extremism*, 194.

5   Griffin here is building on earlier work by George Mosse, who he acknowledges pioneered this approach. Griffin, *Fascism*, 81.

6   Griffin, *Fascism*, 81.

7   Cassam, *Extremism*, 205.

8   Cassam, *Extremism*, 208–209.

9   Nguyen, "Echo Chambers and Epistemic Bubbles," 141.

10   Nguyen, "Echo Chambers and Epistemic Bubbles," 143.

11   Nguyen, "Echo Chambers and Epistemic Bubbles," 145.

12   Nguyen, "Echo Chambers and Epistemic Bubbles," 146.

13   Nguyen, "Echo Chambers and Epistemic Bubbles," 146.

14   Nguyen, "Echo Chambers and Epistemic Bubbles," 150.

15   Nguyen, "Echo Chambers and Epistemic Bubbles," 157.

16   SillyWhabbit, "I Just Heard from My Q."

17   Truthwins24_7, "A Chink in the Q Armour...."

18   Nguyen, "Echo Chambers and Epistemic Bubbles," 158.

19   Kitchen-Count7879, "My Story of Deradicalization and Recovery from the Extreme Far-Right (Long)."

20   Kitchen-Count7879, "My Story of Deradicalization and Recovery from the Extreme Far-Right (Long)."

21   Kitchen-Count7879, "My Story of Deradicalization and Recovery from the Extreme Far-Right (Long)."

22   Roose, "The Making of a YouTube Radical."

23   Loewinger, "How YouTube's Left Is Changing Minds."

24   Hall and Brownstein, "ContraPoints Is the Opposite of the Internet."

25   Draham, "Kill Your Gods!"

26   Draham, "Kill Your Gods!"

27   Draham, "Kill Your Gods!"

28   Kruglanski et al., "The Psychology of Radicalization and Deradicalization," 87.

29   Kruglanski et al., "The Psychology of Radicalization and Deradicalization," 86, 87.

30   Tom Pettinger make this same point, stating that in contemporary programmes that combat radicalization "radical stances that challenge the state's power are solved by the state by re-imposing its hegemony through paternalistic targeting of imprisoned subjects' personal values and political outlook, and rewarding them when 'divergents' align themselves with the state's view of what is acceptable to believe." Pettinger, "De-Radicalization and Counter-Radicalization," 27.

31   Cohn, *The Pursuit of the Millennium.*

References

Ad Fontes Media. "Ad Fontes Media." Ad Fontes Media, 2021. https://adf
ontesmedia.com/.

Ahmed, Sara. "A Phenomenology of Whiteness." *Feminist Theory* 8, no. 2
(2007): 149–68.

———. *Cultural Politics of Emotion*. Edinburgh: Edinburgh University
Press, 2014.

Anglin, Andrew. "A Normies Guide to the Alt-Right." Daily Stormer, August 31, 2016. https://dailystormer.name/a-normies-guide-to-the-a
lt-right/.

———. "Writing Guide." Daily Stormer, 2017. https://www.documentcl
oud.org/documents/4325810-Writers.html.

Angus, Chris. "Radicalisation and Violent Extremism: Causes and Responses." Sydney: NSW Parliamentary Research Service, February
2016.

Anons. "Q: The Basics—An Introduction to Q and the Great Awakening,"
September 19, 2018. https://qanon.news/pdf/Q_The_Basics_V1.0.pd
f.

Appadurai, Arjun. *Fear of Small Numbers*. Durham, NC: Duke University
Press, 2006.

Apter, David. *The Legitimization of Violence*. New York: NYU Press, 1997.

Argentino, Marc-André. "In the Name of the Father, Son, and Q: Why
It's Important to See QAnon as a 'Hyper-Real' Religion." Religion
Dispatches, May 28, 2020. https://religiondispatches.org/in-the-na
me-of-the-father-son-and-q-why-its-important-to-see-qanon-as-
a-hyper-real-religion/.

———. "Pastel QAnon." *Global Network on Extremism and Technology* (blog), March 17, 2021. https://gnet-research.org/2021/03/17/pastel-qanon/.

———. "QAnon and the Storm of the U.S. Capitol: The Offline Effect of Online Conspiracy Theories." The Conversation, January 7, 2021. http://theconversation.com/qanon-and-the-storm-of-the-u-s-capitol-the-offline-effect-of-online-conspiracy-theories-152815.

Barkun, Michael. *A Culture of Conspiracy: Apocalyptic Visions in Contemporary America*. Berkeley: University of California Press, 2013.

Bartlett, Jamie, Jonathan Birdwell, and Mark Littler. "The New Face of Digital Populism." London: Demos, 2011.

Beanz, Tracy. "Tracy Beanz." YouTube, 2020. https://www.youtube.com /c/tracybeanz/about.

Beckett, Lois. "QAnon: A Timeline of Violence Linked to the Conspiracy Theory." *The Guardian*, October 16, 2020, sec. US news. https://www .theguardian.com/us-news/2020/oct/15/qanon-violence-crimes-ti meline.

Beran, Dale. *It Came from Something Awful: How a Toxic Troll Army Accidentally Memed Donald Trump into Office*. New York: All Points Books, 2019.

Berardi, Franco. *Heroes: Mass Murder and Suicide*. London: Verso, 2015.

Berezin, Mabel. *Illiberal Politics in Neoliberal Times*. Cambridge: Cambridge University Press, 2009.

Berkowitz, Reed. "A Game Designer's Analysis Of QAnon." *Curioser Institute* (blog), January 11, 2021. https://medium.com/curiouserinstitute /a-game-designers-analysis-of-qanon-580972548be5.

Berlet, Chip, and Matthew Lyons. *Right-Wing Populism in America: Too Close for Comfort*. Guilford Press, 2000.

Birenboim, Amit. "The Influence of Urban Environments on Our Subjective Momentary Experiences." *Environment and Planning B: Urban Analytics and City Science* 45, no. 5 (September 1, 2018): 915–32. https:/ /doi.org/10.1177/2399808317690149.

BlackPoseidon. "Dad Is Too Far Gone, Thinks I'm Possessed by a Demon." Reddit Post. *R/QAnonCasualties*, October 19, 2021. www.reddi t.com/r/QAnonCasualties/comments/qb5tjl/dad_is_too_far_gone_ thinks_im_possessed_by_a_demon/.

Bloom, Mia, and Sophia Moskalenko. *Pastels and Pedophiles: Inside the Mind of QAnon*. Stanford, CA: Stanford University Press, 2021.

Bomey, Nathan. "Parler, MeWe, Gab Gain Momentum as Conservative Social Media Alternatives in Post-Trump Age." USA TODAY, November 11, 2020. https://www.usatoday.com/story/tech/2020/11/11/parler-mewe-gab-social-media-trump-election-facebook-twitter/6232351002/.

Booeshaghi, Sina. "Want to Mine the #Parler Data Dump? Perform Natural Language Processing (#NLP) on the Content of the Posts? I Made a Video Showing How to Do Exactly That; Cc @parlertakes: Https://T.Co/EFDm2jR4LU." Tweet. *@sinabooeshaghi* (blog), January 12, 2021. https://twitter.com/sinabooeshaghi/status/1349051429999108096.

Borgeson, Kevin, and Robin Valeri. "Faces of Hate." *Journal of Applied Sociology* os-21, no. 2 (September 2004): 99–111. https://doi.org/10.1177/19367244042100205.

Bosker, Bianca. "The Binge Breaker." *The Atlantic*, November 2016. https://www.theatlantic.com/magazine/archive/2016/11/the-binge-breaker/501122/.

Boyd, Danah. "Social Network Sites as Networked Publics: Affordances, Dynamics, and Implications." In *A Networked Self*, 47–66. Routledge, 2010.

Brandt, Libertina, and Grace Dean. "Gab, a Social-Networking Site Popular among the Far Right, Seems to Be Capitalising on Twitter Bans and Parler Being Forced Offline. It Says It's Gaining 10,000 New Users an Hour." *Business Insider* (blog), January 11, 2021. https://www.businessinsider.com.au/gab-reports-growth-in-the-midst-of-twitter-bans-2021-1.

Bruns, Axel, and Jean Burgess. "Twitter Hashtags from Ad Hoc to Calculated Publics." *Hashtag Publics: The Power and Politics of Discursive Networks*, 2015, 13–28.

Bruns, Axel, Brenda Moon, Avijit Paul, and Felix Münch. "Towards a Typology of Hashtag Publics: A Large-Scale Comparative Study of User Engagement across Trending Topics." *Communication Research and Practice* 2, no. 1 (2016): 20–46.

Cameron, Dell, and Dhruv Mehrotra. "Parler Users Breached Deep In-side U.S. Capitol Building, GPS Data Shows." Gizmodo, January 12, 2021. https://gizmodo.com/parler-users-breached-deep-inside-u-s-capitol-building-1846042905.

Camus, Renaud. *Le grand remplacement*. Paris: Reinharc, 2011.

———. *You Will Not Replace Us!* Paris: Chez l'auteur, 2018.

Carroll, John, and David Karpf. "How Can Social Media Firms Tackle Hate Speech?" Knowledge@Wharton, September 22, 2018. https://knowledge.wharton.upenn.edu/article/can-social-media-firms-tackle-hate-speech/.

Cassam, Quassim. *Extremism: A Philosophical Analysis*. London: Routledge, 2021.

Castle, Taimi. "'Cops and the Klan': Police Disavowal of Risk and Minimization of Threat from the Far-Right." *Critical Criminology*, 2020, 1–21.

Chandrasekharan, Eshwar, Umashanthi Pavalanathan, Anirudh Srinivasan, Adam Glynn, Jacob Eisenstein, and Eric Gilbert. "You Can't Stay Here: The Efficacy of Reddit's 2015 Ban Examined Through Hate Speech." *Proceedings of the ACM on Human-Computer Interaction* 1, no. CSCW (December 6, 2017): 1–22. https://doi.org/10.1145/3134666.

Cheah, Kit Sun. "The Current State of Alt-Tech." Steemit, September 20, 2017. https://steemit.com/technology/@cheah/the-current-state-of-alt-tech.

Chetty, Naganna, and Sreejith Alathur. "Hate Speech Review in the Context of Online Social Networks." *Aggression and Violent Behavior* 40, no. May-June 2018 (May 1, 2018): 108–18. https://doi.org/10.1016/j.avb.2018.05.003.

Chun, Wendy Hui Kyong. "Queerying Homophily." In *Pattern Discrimination*, edited by Clemens Apprich, Wendy Hui Kyong Chun, Florian Cramer, and Hito Steyerl, 59–97. Lüneburg, Germany: Meson Press, 2018. https://mediarep.org/handle/doc/13259.

Coates, Ta-Nehisi. *We Were Eight Years in Power: An American Tragedy*. New York: One World, 2017.

Cobb, Jelani. "Inside the Trial of Dylann Roof." *The New Yorker*, January 29, 2017. http://www.newyorker.com/magazine/2017/02/06/inside-the-trial-of-dylann-roof.

Cohen, Anthony. *Symbolic Construction of Community*. London: Ellis Harwood and Tavistock, 1985.

Cohn, Norman. *The Pursuit of the Millennium: Revolutionary Millenarians and Mystical Anarchists of the Middle Ages*. New York: Random House, 1957.

Collins, Ben. "What Is Qanon? A Guide to the Conspiracy Theory Taking Hold among Trump Supporters." NBC News, August 4, 2018. h ttps://www.nbcnews.com/tech/tech-news/what-qanon-guide-cons piracy-theory-taking-hold-among-trump-supporters-n897271.

Conlon, Catherine, Virpi Timonen, Catherine Elliott-O'Dare, Sorcha O' Keeffe, and Geraldine Foley. "Confused About Theoretical Sampling? Engaging Theoretical Sampling in Diverse Grounded Theory Studies." *Qualitative Health Research* 30 (January 20, 2020): 104973231989913. https://doi.org/10.1177/1049732319899139.

Couldry, Nick. "Alternative Media and Mediated Community." In *International Association for Media and Communication Research, Barcelona*. Barcelona, 2002.

Crenshaw, Kimberle. "Demarginalizing the Intersection of Race and Sex: A Black Feminist Critique of Antidiscrimination Doctrine, Feminist Theory and Antiracist Politics," 140:139, 1989.

Culliford, Elizabeth, and Katie Paul. "Unhappy with Twitter, Thousands of Saudis Join pro-Trump Social Network Parler." *Reuters*, June 13, 2019, sec. Media and Telecoms. https://www.reuters.com/article/u s-twitter-saudi-politics-idUSKCN1TE32S.

Dalgaard-Nielsen, Anja. "Violent Radicalization in Europe: What We Know and What We Do Not Know." *Studies in Conflict & Terrorism* 33, no. 9 (August 16, 2010): 797–814. https://doi.org/10.1080/1057610X.2 010.501423.

Damasio, Manuel Jos, Sara Henriques, and Conceio Costa. "Belonging to a Community: The Mediation of Belonging." *Observatorio*, Special Issue (2012): 20.

Dangerous Speech Project. "FAQ." Dangerous Speech Project, October 27, 2016. https://dangerousspeech.org/faq/.

deleted. "It's Really Only a Matter of Time until I Become Estranged with Q Family and I Just Wonder When It's Gonna Come." Reddit Post. *R/QAnonCasualties*, October 18, 2021. www.reddit.com/r/QAnonCasualties/comments/qat3gt/its_really_only_a_matter_of_time_until_i_become/.

Deleuze, Gilles. *Nietzsche and Philosophy*. Columbia University Press, 2006.

Demby, Gene, and Shereen Marisol Meraji. "From The Fringe To The Capitol." Code Switch. Accessed September 24, 2021. https://www.npr.org/2021/01/11/955673514/from-the-fringe-to-the-capitol.

Devine, Nesta. "Beyond Truth and Non-Truth." In *Post-Truth, Fake News*, edited by Michael Peters, Sharon Rider, and Tina Besley, 161–68. Singapore: Springer, 2018.

Diceblue. "R/QAnonCasualties—I'm an Ex Q, Former Conspiracy Theorist, Ama." Reddit, February 22, 2021. https://www.reddit.com/r/QAnonCasualties/comments/l3yhqc/im_an_ex_q_former_conspiracy_theorist_ama/.

Diken, Bulent. *Nihilism*. Routledge, 2008.

Djuric, Nemanja, Jing Zhou, Robin Morris, Mihajlo Grbovic, Vladan Radosavljevic, and Narayan Bhamidipati. "Hate Speech Detection with Comment Embeddings." In *Proceedings of the 24th International Conference on World Wide Web*, 29–30. WWW '15 Companion. Florence, Italy: Association for Computing Machinery, 2015. https://doi.org/10.1145/2740908.2742760.

Donk_enby. "Crash Override (@donk_enby) / Twitter." Twitter, 2021. https://twitter.com/donk_enby.

Donovan, Joan, Becca Lewis, and Brian Friedberg. "Parallel Ports: Sociotechnical Change from the Alt-Right to Alt-Tech." In *Post-Digital Cultures of the Far Right*, edited by Maik Fielitz and Nick Thurston, 49–66. Bielefeld: transcript Verlag, 2019.

Draham, Jesse. "QAnon." Kill Your Gods. Accessed November 15, 2021. https://ihateinfinitejest.libsyn.com/qanon-casualties-w-mike-rains.

Ebner, Julia. "Replatforming Unreality." *Journal of Design and Science*, no. 6 (September 5, 2019). https://doi.org/10.21428/7808da6b.e585ddcb.

Ehrenkranz, Melanie. "Gab, a Haven for White Nationalists, Is Now Trying to Reach Young, Diverse Progressives." Mic, March 18, 2017. https://www.mic.com/articles/171268/gab-a-haven-for-white-nationalists-is-now-trying-to-reach-young-diverse-progressives.

Ellinas, Antonis A. *The Media and the Far Right in Western Europe: Playing the Nationalist Card*. Cambridge, UK: Cambridge University Press, 2010.

Energy.gov. "Departmental Personnel Security FAQs." Energy.gov, 2020. https://www.energy.gov/ehss/security-policy-guidance-reports/departmental-personnel-security-faqs.

Engels, Jeremy. *The Politics of Resentment*. University Park, PA: Penn State University Press, 2021.

Eylar, Alex. "How I Fell Down the QAnon Rabbit Hole (As Told by Those Still Inside It)." Tweet. *@alexandereylar* (blog), August 18, 2021. https://twitter.com/alexandereylar/status/1428113363058397187.

Facebook. "Mark Zuckerberg Status Update," November 18, 2016. https://www.facebook.com/zuck/posts/10103269806149061.

Fan, Rui, Ke Xu, and Jichang Zhao. "Higher Contagion and Weaker Ties Mean Anger Spreads Faster than Joy in Social Media." *ArXiv:1608.03656 [Physics]*, August 11, 2016. http://arxiv.org/abs/1608.03656.

Fang, Lee, and Leighton Akio Woodhouse. "How White Nationalism Became Normal Online." *The Intercept* (blog), August 25, 2017. https://theintercept.com/2017/08/25/video-how-white-nationalism-became-normal-online/.

Farkas, Johan, and Christina Neumayer. "Mimicking News: How the Credibility of an Established Tabloid Is Used When Disseminating Racism." *Nordicom Review* 41, no. 1 (January 19, 2020): 1–17. https://doi.org/10.2478/nor-2020-0001.

Feeld, Julian. "Texas QAnon Supporter Used Car to Attack Strangers She Believed Were 'Pedophiles.'" Right Wing Watch, August 20, 2020. https://www.rightwingwatch.org/post/texas-qanon-car-attack-cecilia-fulbright/.

Feffer, John. "Nationalism Is Global. The Left Is on the Defensive.," November 6, 2019. https://www.thenation.com/article/archive/far-right-nationalist-climate-crisis/.

Feldman, Matthew. "Between Alt-Right and Mainstream Conservatism: The 'Near Right' in Contemporary American Politics and Culture." Unpublished, 2017.

———. "Terrorist's Creed by Roger Griffin." *Modernism/Modernity* 20, no. 3 (2013): 594–97. https://doi.org/10.1353/mod.2013.0067.

Fenster, Mark. *Conspiracy Theories: Secrecy and Power in Contemporary America*. Minneapolis: University of Minnesota Press, 2008.

Feola, Michael. "'You Will Not Replace Us': The Melancholic Nationalism of Whiteness." *Political Theory* 49, no. 4 (2021): 528–53.

Fielitz, Maik, and Holger Marcks. "Digital Fascism: Challenges for the Open Society in Times of Social Media." Berkeley: Center for Right Wing Studies, July 16, 2019. https://escholarship.org/uc/item/87w5c5gp.

———. *Digitaler Faschismus: Die Sozialen Medien Als Motor Des Rechtsextremismus*. Berlin: Duden Verlag, 2020.

Finley, Stephen C, Biko Mandela Gray, and Lori Latrice Martin. "'The Souls of White Folk': Race, Affect, and Religion in the Religion of White Rage." In *The Religion of White Rage: White Workers, Religious Fervor, and the Myth of Black Racial Progress*, 1–27. Edinburgh: Edinburgh University Press, 2020.

Fisher, Max, and Amanda Taub. "How Everyday Social Media Users Become Real-World Extremists." *The New York Times*, October 10, 2018, sec. World. https://www.nytimes.com/2018/04/25/world/asia/facebook-extremism.html.

Fleming, Andy, and Aurelien Mondon. "The Radical Right in Australia." In *The Oxford Handbook of the Radical Right*, edited by Jens Rydgren, 917–39. Oxford: Oxford University Press, 2018.

Foley, Katherine Ellen. "Pittsburgh Suspect Robert Bowers Wrote Anti-Semitic and Racist Posts on Social Media." Quartz, October 28, 2018. https://qz.com/1440746/pittsburgh-suspect-robert-bowers-had-anti-semitic-and-racist-posts-on-social-media/.

Fortuna, Paula, and Sérgio Nunes. "A Survey on Automatic Detection of Hate Speech in Text." *ACM Computing Surveys (CSUR)* 51, no. 4 (2018): 1–30.

Foss, Sonja K. *Rhetorical Criticism: Exploration and Practice*. Long Grove, IL: Waveland Press, 2017.

Foucault, Michel. "Prison Talk." In *Power/Knowledge: Selected Interviews and Other Writings, 1972–1977*, edited by Colin Gordon, 37–54. New York: Pantheon, 1980.

Frenkel, Sheera, and Zolan Kanno-Yungs. "How They Stormed Congress." The Daily, January 8, 2021. https://www.stitcher.co m/show/the-daily-10/episode/how-they-stormed-congress-80680 063.

Fuchs, Christian. *Digital Demagogue: Authoritarian Capitalism in the Age of Trump and Twitter*. London, UK: Pluto Press, 2018. https://doi.org/10 .2307/j.ctt21215dw.

FucknOathMate. "Message from FucknOathMate in Vibrant Diversity #general." *Unicorn Riot: Discord Leaks*, January 29, 2017. https://discor dleaks.unicornriot.ninja/discord/view/754755?q=red+pilled#msg.

Gab. "Gab." StartEngine, 2017. https://www.startengine.com/gab.

———. "Gab Social." Gab Social hosted on gab.com, 2020. https://gab.c om/.

Gab AI. "Dissenter | Free Speech Web Browser," 2019. https://dissenter. com.

———. "Frequently Asked Questions." Dissenter, 2019. https://dissenter .com.

———. "Gab Apps," 2020. https://apps.gab.com.

Garis, Roy. *Immigration Restriction: A Study of the Opposition to and Regula-tion of Immigration into the United States*. New York: Macmillan, 1927.

Garry, Amanda, Samantha Walther, Rukaya Mohamed, and Ayan Mo-hammed. "QAnon Conspiracy Theory: Examining Its Evolution and Mechanisms of Radicalization," 2021, 65.

Garsd, Jasmine. "Free Speech Or Hate Speech: When Does On-line Hate Speech Become A Real Threat?" *NPR*, November 19, 2018. https://www.npr.org/2018/11/19/669361577/free-speech-or-hat e-speech-when-does-online-hate-speech-become-a-real-threat.

Gershon, Ilana. "Neoliberal Agency." *Current Anthropology* 52, no. 4 (2011): 537–55.

Gilbert, David. "Here's How Big Far Right Social Network Gab Has Actually Gotten." *Vice* (blog), August 16, 2019. https://www.vice.com /en_us/article/pa7dwg/heres-how-big-far-right-social-network-ga b-has-actually-gotten.

———. "Users of Far-Right Social Network Gab Can Now Comment on the Entire Internet." *Vice* (blog), February 27, 2019. https://www.vice .com/en_us/article/nexq9d/gab-far-right-social-network-commen ts.

Gillespie, Tarleton. "Platforms Intervene." *Social Media + Society* 1, no. 1 (April 29, 2015): 205630511558047. https://doi.org/10.1177/2056305115 580479.

Glennon, Seána. "The Anti-Mask Movement and the Rise of the Right in Ireland: What Does It Mean for Our Democracy?" IACL-IADC Blog, January 12, 2021. https://blog-iacl-aidc.org/2021-posts/2021/1/12/th e-anti-mask-movement-and-the-rise-of-the-right-in-ireland-wha t-does-it-mean-for-our-democracy.

Goel, Vindu. "Facebook Tinkers With Users' Emotions in News Feed Experiment, Stirring Outcry." *The New York Times*, June 30, 2014, sec. Technology. https://www.nytimes.com/2014/06/30/technology/face book-tinkers-with-users-emotions-in-news-feed-experiment-stirr ing-outcry.html.

Goldman, David. "Big Tech Made the Social Media Mess. It Has to Fix It." CNN, October 29, 2018. https://www.cnn.com/2018/10/29/tech/soci al-media-hate-speech/index.html.

Goodwin, Megan. QAnon Didn't Just Spring Forth From the Void — It's the Latest From a Familiar Movement. Interview by Adam Willems, September 10, 2020. https://religiondispatches.org/qanon-didnt-ju st-spring-forth-from-the-void-its-the-latest-from-a-familiar-mov ement/.

Gottfried, Paul. "The Decline and Rise of the Alternative Right." *Taki's Magazine*, 2008. http://takimag.com/article/the_decline_and_rise_ of_the_alternative_right/print#axzz4InOGAwpd.

Graham, Jesse, and Jonathan Haidt. "Beyond Beliefs: Religions Bind Individuals Into Moral Communities." *Personality and Social Psychology
Review* 14, no. 1 (February 1, 2010): 140–50. https://doi.org/10.1177/10
88868309353415.

Gray, John. *Straw Dogs: Thoughts on Humans and Other Animals.* New York:
Farrar, Straus and Giroux, 2016.

Griffin, Roger. *Fascism: Key Concepts in Political Theory.* London: Polity,
2018.

———. "Modernity, Modernism, and Fascism: A 'Mazeway Resynthesis.'"
Modernism/Modernity 15, no. 1 (2008): 9–24. https://doi.org/10.1353/m
od.2008.0011.

———. *Terrorist's Creed: Fanatical Violence and the Human Need for Meaning.*
London: Springer, 2012.

Groeger, Lena, Jeff Kao, Al Shaw, Moiz Syed, and Maya Eliahou. "What
Parler Saw During the Attack on the Capitol." ProPublica, January 17,
2021. https://projects.propublica.org/parler-capitol-videos/.

Grossman, Lev. "You — Yes, You — Are TIME's Person of the Year." *Time,*
December 25, 2006. http://content.time.com/time/magazine/articl
e/0,9171,1570810,00.html.

Guynn, Jessica. "'Massive Rise' in Hate Speech on Twitter during Presidential Election." USA TODAY, October 26, 2016. https://www.usato
day.com/story/tech/news/2016/10/21/massive-rise-in-hate-speech-
twitter-during-presidential-election-donald-trump/92486210/.

Habermas, Jürgen. *An Awareness of What Is Missing: Faith and Reason in a
Post-Secular Age.* London: Polity, 2010.

Hall, Jake, and Billie Brownstein. "ContraPoints Is the Opposite of the
Internet," September 4, 2019. https://www.vice.com/en/article/qvyg
kv/contrapoints-interview-2019-natalie-wynn.

Haney-López, Ian. *Dog Whistle Politics: How Coded Racial Appeals Have Reinvented Racism and Wrecked the Middle Class.* Oxford, UK: Oxford University Press, 2015.

Hannah, Matthew. "QAnon and the Information Dark Age." *First Monday,*
January 15, 2021. https://doi.org/10.5210/fm.v26i2.10868.

Harambam, Jaron, and Stef Aupers. "Contesting Epistemic Authority:
Conspiracy Theories on the Boundaries of Science." *Public Under-*

standing of Science 24, no. 4 (May 1, 2015): 466–80. https://doi.org/10 .1177/0963662514559891.

Hartzell, Stephanie L. "Alt-White: Conceptualizing the 'Alt-Right' as a Rhetorical Bridge between White Nationalism and Mainstream Public Discourse." *Journal of Contemporary Rhetoric* 8 (2018).

Hawes, Jennifer Berry. "Dylann Roof Jailhouse Journal." *Post and Courier*, January 5, 2017. https://www.postandcourier.com/dylann-roof-jail house-journal/pdf_da3e19b8-d3b3-11e6-b040-03089263e67c.html.

Hawley, George. *The Alt-Right: What Everyone Needs to Know®*. Oxford: Oxford University Press, 2018.

Heilweil, Rebecca. "Parler, the 'Free Speech' Social Network, Explained." *Vox*, November 24, 2020. https://www.vox.com/recode/2020/11/24/ 21579357/parler-app-trump-twitter-facebook-censorship.

Heinkelmann-Wild, Tim, Lisa Kriegmair, Berthold Rittberger, and Bernhard Zangl. "Divided They Fail: The Politics of Wedge Issues and Brexit." *Journal of European Public Policy* 27, no. 5 (May 3, 2020): 723–41. https://doi.org/10.1080/13501763.2019.1683058.

Hochschild, Arlie Russell. *Strangers in Their Own Land: Anger and Mourning on the American Right*. New York: The New Press, 2018.

Hoppa, Kristin. "Affidavit: Drunk Driver Who Rammed Car Claimed to Be Chasing Pedophile." WacoTrib.com. Accessed September 17, 2021. https://wacotrib.com/news/local/crime-and-courts/affidavit-drunk-driver-who-rammed-car-claimed-to-be-chasing-pedophile /article_5989fa98-49fb-5db1-a5f2-2cef7a42e009.html.

Horgan, John. *The Psychology of Terrorism*. London: Routledge, 2004.

Horwitz, Jeff, and Keach Hagey. "Parler CEO Says He Was Fired as Platform Neared Restoring Service." *Wall Street Journal*, February 4, 2021, sec. Tech. https://www.wsj.com/articles/parler-ceo-says-he-was-fi red-by-conservative-political-donor-rebekah-mercer-11612397380.

———. "Parler Makes Play for Conservatives Mad at Facebook, Twitter." *Wall Street Journal*, November 15, 2020, sec. Tech. https://www.wsj.c om/articles/parler-backed-by-mercer-family-makes-play-for-cons ervatives-mad-at-facebook-twitter-11605382430.

Ingrams, Alex. "Connective Action and the Echo Chamber of Ideology: Testing a Model of Social Media Use and Attitudes toward the Role of

Government." *Journal of Information Technology & Politics* 14, no. 1 (January 2, 2017): 1–15. https://doi.org/10.1080/19331681.2016.1261264.

Jacobs, Jane. *The Death and Life of Great American Cities*. Reissue edition. New York: Vintage, 1992.

Jasko, Katarzyna, Gary LaFree, and Arie Kruglanski. "Quest for Significance and Violent Extremism: The Case of Domestic Radicalization." *Political Psychology* 38, no. 5 (2017): 815–31.

Jasser, Greta, Jordan McSwiney, Ed Pertwee, and Savvas Zannettou. "'Welcome to #GabFam': Far-Right Virtual Community on Gab." *New Media & Society*, June 28, 2021, 14614448211024546. https://doi.org/10.1177/14614448211024546.

Jett, Brandon, and Allison Robinson. "The Chilling Similarities between the Pro-Trump Mob and Lynchings a Century Ago." *Washington Post*, January 15, 2021. https://www.washingtonpost.com/outlook/2021/01/15/chilling-similarities-between-pro-trump-mob-lynchings-century-ago/.

Johnson, Jenna. "Trump Gathers with Military Leaders, Says 'Maybe It's the Calm before the Storm.'" *Washington Post*, October 6, 2017. https://www.washingtonpost.com/news/post-politics/wp/2017/10/06/trump-gathers-with-military-leaders-says-maybe-its-the-calm-before-the-storm/.

Johnson, Martenzie. "The Storming of the U.S. Capitol Is What Happens When White Supremacy Is Coddled." *The Undefeated* (blog), January 11, 2021. https://theundefeated.com/features/the-storming-of-us-capitol-is-what-happens-when-white-supremacy-is-coddled/.

Johnston, Chris. "The Vow." Text. The Saturday Paper, October 3, 2020. https://www.thesaturdaypaper.com.au/culture/television/2020/10/03/the-vow/160164720010504.

Jung, Moon-Kie. "Constituting the Us Empire-State and White Supremacy: The Early Years." In *State of White Supremacy*, 1–24. Stanford, CA: Stanford University Press, 2020.

Kalmar, Ivan, Christopher Stevens, and Nicholas Worby. "Twitter, Gab, and Racism: The Case of the Soros Myth." In *Proceedings of the 9th International Conference on Social Media and Society*, 330–34. SMSociety

'18. Copenhagen, Denmark: Association for Computing Machinery, 2018. https://doi.org/10.1145/3217804.3217939.

Kant, Immanuel. "Beantwortung Der Frage: Was Ist Aufklärung?" *Berlinische Monatsschrift*, December 1784.

Karell, Daniel, and Michael Freedman. "Rhetorics of Radicalism." *American Sociological Review* 84, no. 4 (August 1, 2019): 726–53. https://doi.o rg/10.1177/0003122419859519.

Kashima, Yoshihisa, Andrew Perfors, Vanessa Ferdinand, and Elle Pattenden. "Ideology, Communication and Polarization." *Philosophical Transactions of the Royal Society B: Biological Sciences* 376, no. 1822 (April 12, 2021): 20200133. https://doi.org/10.1098/rstb.2020.0133.

Kaye, David. "Governments and Internet Companies Fail to Meet Challenges of Online Hate—UN Expert." OHCHR, October 9, 2019. https://www.ohchr.org/EN/NewsEvents/Pages/DisplayNews. aspx?NewsID=25174&LangID=E.

Killgore, William D. S., Sara A. Cloonan, Emily C. Taylor, and Natalie S. Dailey. "Loneliness: A Signature Mental Health Concern in the Era of COVID-19." *Psychiatry Research* 290 (August 1, 2020): 113117. https://d oi.org/10.1016/j.psychres.2020.113117.

King, Martin Luther. *Where Do We Go from Here: Chaos or Community?* Boston: Beacon Press, 1968.

King, Nigel. "Using Templates in the Thematic Analysis of Text." In *Essential Guide to Qualitative Methods in Organizational Research*, edited by Catherine Cassell and Gillian Symon, 256–70. London: Sage, 2004.

Kitchen-Count7879. "My Story of Deradicalization and Recovery from the Extreme Far-Right (Long)." Reddit Post. *R/ReQovery*, November 3, 2021. www.reddit.com/r/ReQovery/comments/qly1jn/my_story_ of_deradicalization_and_recovery_from/.

Knapton, Sarah. "Rise of the Anti-Maskers: The Psychology of Why Face Coverings Are Causing so Much Upset." *The Telegraph*, July 27, 2020. https://www.telegraph.co.uk/news/2020/07/27/rise-anti-ma skers-psychology-face-coverings-causing-much-upset/.

Koehler, Daniel. *Understanding Deradicalization: Methods, Tools and Programs for Countering Violent Extremism*. Routledge, 2016.

Kruglanski, Arie W, Xiaoyan Chen, Mark Dechesne, Shira Fishman, and Edward Orehek. "Fully Committed: Suicide Bombers' Motivation and the Quest for Personal Significance." *Political Psychology* 30, no. 3 (2009): 331–57.

Kruglanski, Arie W, Michele J Gelfand, Jocelyn J Bélanger, Anna Sheveland, Malkanthi Hetiarachchi, and Rohan Gunaratna. "The Psychology of Radicalization and Deradicalization: How Significance Quest Impacts Violent Extremism." *Political Psychology* 35 (2014): 69–93.

Kruglanski, Arie W., Michele J. Gelfand, Jocelyn J. Bélanger, Anna Sheveland, Malkanthi Hetiarachchi, and Rohan Gunaratna. "The Psychology of Radicalization and Deradicalization: How Significance Quest Impacts Violent Extremism: Processes of Radicalization and Deradicalization." *Political Psychology* 35 (February 2014): 69–93. https://doi.org/10.1111/pops.12163.

LaFrance, Adrienne. "The Prophecies of Q." The Atlantic, May 14, 2020. https://www.theatlantic.com/magazine/archive/2020/06/qanon-nothing-can-stop-what-is-coming/610567/.

———. "The Prophecies of Q." *The Atlantic*, June 2020. https://www.theatlantic.com/magazine/archive/2020/06/qanon-nothing-can-stop-what-is-coming/610567/.

Lalich, Janja. *Bounded Choice: True Believers and Charismatic Cults*. Berkeley, CA: University of California Press, 2004.

Landreville, Kristen D., and Cassie Niles. "'And That's a Fact!': The Roles of Political Ideology, PSRs, and Perceived Source Credibility in Estimating Factual Content in Partisan News." *Journal of Broadcasting & Electronic Media* 63, no. 2 (April 3, 2019): 177–94. https://doi.org/10.1080/08838151.2019.1622339.

Lantian, Anthony, Virginie Bagneux, Sylvain Delouvée, and Nicolas Gauvrit. "Maybe Free Thinker but Not a Critical One: High Conspiracy Belief Is Associated with Low Critical Thinking Ability," 2020.

Lavin, Talia. "QAnon, Blood Libel, and the Satanic Panic." *The New Republic*, September 30, 2020. https://newrepublic.com/article/159529/qanon-blood-libel-satanic-panic.

Lee, Micah. "Inside Gab, the Online Safe Space for Far-Right Extremists." *The Intercept* (blog), March 15, 2021. https://theintercept.com/2021/0 3/15/gab-hack-donald-trump-parler-extremists/.

Lehman, Joseph G. "An Introduction to the Overton Window of Political Possibility." Midland, MI: Mackinac Center for Public Policy, 2010. h ttps://www.mackinac.org/12481.

Lewis, Paul. "'Our Minds Can Be Hijacked': The Tech Insiders Who Fear a Smartphone Dystopia." *The Guardian*, October 6, 2017. http://www .theguardian.com/technology/2017/oct/05/smartphone-addiction-silicon-valley-dystopia.

Lifton, Robert Jay. *Thought Reform and the Psychology of Totalism: A Study of "Brainwashing" in China*. Chapel Hill: University of North Carolina Press, 2012.

Lima, Cristiano. "Cruz Joins Alternative Social Media Site Parler in Swipe at Big Tech Platforms." POLITICO, June 25, 2020. https://www.polit ico.com/news/2020/06/25/ted-cruz-joins-parler-339811.

Lima, Lucas, Julio C. S. Reis, Philipe Melo, Fabricio Murai, Leandro Araújo, Pantelis Vikatos, and Fabrício Benevenuto. "Inside the Right-Leaning Echo Chambers: Characterizing Gab, an Unmoderated Social System." *ArXiv:1807.03688 [Cs]*, July 10, 2018. http://arxiv.org/ab s/1807.03688.

Loewinger, Micah. "How YouTube's Left Is Changing Minds." On the Media. Accessed November 15, 2021. https://www.wnycstudios.org/pod casts/otm/segments/how-youtubes-left-changing-minds.

Lopez, German. "Donald Trump's Long History of Racism, from the 1970s to 2020." Vox, July 25, 2016. https://www.vox.com/2016/7/25/ 12270880/donald-trump-racist-racism-history.

Lourens, Mariné. "Mobs, Violence and Coups: The Power of Online Harassment." Stuff, January 16, 2021. https://www.stuff.co.nz/nati onal/123957282/mobs-violence-and-coups-the-power-of-online-ha rassment.

Mac, Tatiana. "Canary in a Coal Mine: How Tech Provides Platforms for Hate." *A List Apart* (blog), March 19, 2019. https://alistapart.com/artic le/canary-in-a-coal-mine-how-tech-provides-platforms-for-hate/.

Mak, Aaron. "Update: Sheriff Says 'No Known Ties' Between Florida Shooter and White Supremacist Group." *Slate*, February 15, 2018. https://slate.com/news-and-politics/2018/02/law-enforcement-reports-no-known-ties-between-nikolas-cruz-and-white-supremacist-group-republic-of-florida.html.

Mander, J. Sentencing Remarks (2020). https://www.courtsofnz.govt.nz/assets/cases/R-v-Tarrant-sentencing-remarks-20200827.pdf.

Manea, Elham. "Defining the Phenomenon of Jihadist Radicalisation: Drivers and Catalysts Local & Global." Brussels: European Policy Centre, 2017. https://doi.org/10.5167/uzh-179912.

Marcks, Holger, and Janina Pawelz. "From Myths of Victimhood to Fantasies of Violence: How Far-Right Narratives of Imperilment Work." *Terrorism and Political Violence* 0, no. 0 (July 24, 2020): 1–18. https://doi.org/10.1080/09546553.2020.1788544.

Martineau, Paris. "The Storm Is the New Pizzagate — Only Worse." *Intelligencer*, December 19, 2017. https://nymag.com/intelligencer/2017/12/qanon-4chan-the-storm-conspiracy-explained.html.

Martinot, Steve. *The Machinery of Whiteness: Studies in the Structure of Racialization*. Philadelphia, PA: Temple University Press, 2010.

Marwick, Alice, and Rebecca Lewis. "Media Manipulation and Disinformation Online." New York: Data & Society, 2017. https://datasociety.net/pubs/oh/DataAndSociety_MediaManipulationAndDisinformationOnline.pdf.

Matamoros-Fernández, Ariadna. "Platformed Racism: The Mediation and Circulation of an Australian Race-Based Controversy on Twitter, Facebook and YouTube." *Information, Communication & Society* 20, no. 6 (June 3, 2017): 930–46. https://doi.org/10.1080/1369118X.2017.1293130.

Mathew, Binny, Ritam Dutt, Pawan Goyal, and Animesh Mukherjee. "Spread of Hate Speech in Online Social Media." In *Proceedings of the 10th ACM Conference on Web Science*, 173–82. WebSci '19. Boston, Massachusetts, USA: Association for Computing Machinery, 2019. https://doi.org/10.1145/3292522.3326034.

May, Rob, and Matthew Feldman. "Understanding the Alt-Right: Ideologues, 'Lulz' and Hiding in Plain Sight." In *Post-Digital Cultures of the*

Far Right: Online Actions and Offline Consequences in Europe and the US, edited by Maik Fielitz and Nick Thurston, 25–36. Bielefeld, Germany: transcript Verlag, 2018. https://doi.org/10.14361/9783839446706.

McCauley, Clark, and Susan Jacques. "The Popularity of Conspiracy Theories of Presidential Assassination: A Bayesian Analysis." *Journal of Personality and Social Psychology* 37, no. 5 (1979): 637.

McCauley, Clark, and Sophia Moskalenko. *Friction: How Radicalization Happens to Them and Us*. Oxford: Oxford University Press, 2011.

McIlroy-Young, Reid, and Ashton Anderson. "From 'Welcome New Gabbers' to the Pittsburgh Synagogue Shooting: The Evolution of Gab." In *ICWSM*, 13:651–54, 2019.

Media Bias Fact Check. "Media Bias/Fact Check—Search and Learn the Bias of News Media." Media Bias/Fact Check, 2020. https://mediabiasfactcheck.com/.

Melley, Timothy. *Empire of Conspiracy: The Culture of Paranoia in Postwar America*. Ithaca, N.Y: Cornell University Press, 2016.

Mezzofiore, Gianluca, and Donie O'Sullivan. "El Paso Shooting Is at Least the Third Atrocity Linked to 8chan This Year." CNN, August 5, 2019. https://www.cnn.com/2019/08/04/business/el-paso-shooting-8chan-biz/index.html.

Mieville, China. *The City & The City*. New York: Del Rey, 2009.

Mills, Charles W. *The Racial Contract*. Ithaca, NY: Cornell University Press, 1997.

Minkenberg, Michael. *The Radical Right in Europe: An Overview*. Verlag Bertelsmann Stiftung, 2011.

Morozov, Evgeny. "After the Facebook Scandal It's Time to Base the Digital Economy on Public v Private Ownership of Data." *The Observer*, March 31, 2018, sec. Technology. https://www.theguardian.com/technology/2018/mar/31/big-data-lie-exposed-simply-blaming-facebook-wont-fix-reclaim-private-information.

———. "Socialize the Data Centres!" *New Left Review*, II, no. 91 (2015): 45–66.

Mudde, Cas. *The Far Right Today*. London: Polity, 2019.

Munn, Luke. "Alt-Right Pipeline: Individual Journeys to Extremism On-line." *First Monday* 24, no. 6 (June 1, 2019). https://doi.org/10.5210/fm.v24i6.10108.

———. "Angry by Design: Toxic Communication and Technical Architectures." *Humanities and Social Sciences Communications* 7, no. 1 (July 30, 2020): 1–11. https://doi.org/10.1057/s41599-020-00550-7.

———. *Logic of Feeling: Technology's Quest to Capitalize Emotion.* London: Rowman & Littlefield International, 2020.

———. "More than a Mob: Parler as Preparatory Media for the U.S. Capitol Storming." *First Monday* 26, no. 3 (February 7, 2021). https://doi.org/10.5210/fm.v26i3.11574.

Murray, Jennifer L. "The Role of Sexual, Sadistic, and Misogynistic Fantasy in Mass and Serial Killing." *Deviant Behavior* 38, no. 7 (July 3, 2017): 735–43. https://doi.org/10.1080/01639625.2016.1197669.

———. "The Transcendent Fantasy in Mass Killers." *Deviant Behavior* 38, no. 10 (October 3, 2017): 1172–85. https://doi.org/10.1080/01639625.2016.1246015.

Newman, Barbara M., Brenda J. Lohman, and Philip R. Newman. "Peer Group Membership and a Sense of Belonging: Their Relationship to Adolescent Behavior Problems." *Adolescence* 42, no. 166 (2007): 241–63.

Nguyen, C. Thi. "Echo Chambers and Epistemic Bubbles." *Episteme* 17, no. 2 (June 2020): 141–61. http://dx.doi.org.ezproxy.uws.edu.au/10.1017/epi.2018.32.

No Hate. "No Hate Speech Youth Campaign Website." No Hate Speech Youth Campaign. Accessed May 4, 2020. https://www.coe.int/en/web/no-hate-campaign/home.

North, Anna. "How #SaveTheChildren Is Pulling American Moms into QAnon." Vox, September 18, 2020. https://www.vox.com/21436671/save-our-children-hashtag-qanon-pizzagate.

Nyce, Caroline Mimbs. "The Atlantic Daily: QAnon Is a New American Religion." *The Atlantic*, May 14, 2020. https://www.theatlantic.com/newsletters/archive/2020/05/qanon-q-pro-trump-conspiracy/611722/.

Obama, Barack. "President Obama's Farewell Address." January 10, 2017. https://obamawhitehouse.archives.gov/node/360231.

Occeñola, Paige. "8chan Is 'a Cesspool,' 'worst Content on the Internet,' Says Site Founder." Rappler, August 19, 2019. http://www.rappler.co m/technology/news/238066-8chan-fredrick-brennan-shutdown-ra ppler-talk.

Ohlheiser, Abby. "Banned from Twitter? This Site Promises You Can Say Whatever You Want." *Washington Post*, November 30, 2016. https://w ww.washingtonpost.com/news/the-intersect/wp/2016/11/29/banne d-from-twitter-this-site-promises-you-can-say-whatever-you-wa nt/.

———. "Evangelicals Are Looking for Answers Online. They're Finding QAnon Instead." MIT Technology Review, August 26, 2020. https:// www.technologyreview.com/2020/08/26/1007611/how-qanon-is-ta rgeting-evangelicals/.

Owen, Tess. "Gab Is Back in Business after Finding a Payments Proces- sor Willing to Work with the Alt-Right," January 24, 2019. https://w ww.vice.com/en/article/eve43n/gab-is-back-in-business-after-find ing-a-payments-processor-willing-to-work-with-the-alt-right.

Paczkowski, John, and Ryan Mac. "Amazon Is Booting Parler Off Of Its Web Hosting Service." BuzzFeed News, January 9, 2021. https://ww w.buzzfeednews.com/article/johnpaczkowski/amazon-parler-aws.

Pariser, Eli. *The Filter Bubble*. London, UK: Penguin Books, 2012.

Pearson, Adam R., John F. Dovidio, and Samuel L. Gaertner. "The Nature of Contemporary Prejudice: Insights from Aversive Racism." *Social and Personality Psychology Compass* 3, no. 3 (2009): 314–38. https://doi. org/10.1111/j.1751-9004.2009.00183.x.

Penny, Eleanor. "The Deadly Myth of the Great Replacement." *New States- man*, August 9, 2019. https://www.newstatesman.com/politics/2019 /08/the-deadly-myth-of-the-great-replacement.

Pettinger, Tom. "De-Radicalization and Counter-Radicalization: Valu- able Tools Combating Violent Extremism, or Harmful Methods of Subjugation?" *Journal for Deradicalization*, no. 12 (September 14, 2017): 1–59.

Pfeifer, Michael James. *Rough Justice: Lynching and American Society, 1874–1947*. University of Illinois Press, 2004.

Piette, Adam. "Muriel Spark and Fake News." *Textual Practice* 32, no. 9 (October 21, 2018): 1577–91. https://doi.org/10.1080/0950236X.2018.1533 182.

Pita Loor, Karen. "Why a White Mob Felt They Could Storm the US Capitol without Fear." Boston University, January 8, 2021. http://www.bu .edu/articles/2021/why-a-white-mob-could-storm-the-us-capitol/.

Placido, Dani Di. "What I Don't Understand About PewDiePie." *Forbes*, March 31, 2019. https://www.forbes.com/sites/danidiplacido/2019/0 3/31/what-i-dont-understand-about-pewdiepie/.

Praying Medic. "The Coming Global Tsunami." *Praying Medic* (blog), November 8, 2019. https://prayingmedic.com/2019/11/08/the-comin g-global-tsunami/.

Prince, Matthew. "Terminating Service for 8Chan." The Cloudflare Blog, August 5, 2019. https://blog.cloudflare.com/terminating-service-fo r-8chan/.

Procházka, Ondřej, and Jan Blommaert. "Ergoic Framing in New Right Online Groups: Q, the MAGA Kid, and the Deep State Theory." *Australian Review of Applied Linguistics*, June 5, 2020, 1–33. https://doi.org /10.1075/aral.19033.pro.

Prooijen, Jan-Willem van. "Sometimes Inclusion Breeds Suspicion: Self-Uncertainty and Belongingness Predict Belief in Conspiracy Theories." *European Journal of Social Psychology* 46, no. 3 (2016): 267–79. htt ps://doi.org/10.1002/ejsp.2157.

Prooijen, Jan-Willem van, and Michele Acker. "The Influence of Control on Belief in Conspiracy Theories: Conceptual and Applied Extensions." *Applied Cognitive Psychology* 29, no. 5 (2015): 753–61. https://do i.org/10.1002/acp.3161.

Prooijen, Jan-Willem van, and Eric van Dijk. "When Consequence Size Predicts Belief in Conspiracy Theories: The Moderating Role of Perspective Taking." *Journal of Experimental Social Psychology* 55 (November 1, 2014): 63–73. https://doi.org/10.1016/j.jesp.2014.06.006.

qstruggling. "Going Crazy." Reddit Post. *R/ReQovery*, August 27, 2021. w ww.reddit.com/r/ReQovery/comments/pcyd64/going_crazy/.

———. "Trouble Moving On." Reddit Post. *R/ReQovery*, September 13, 2021. www.reddit.com/r/ReQovery/comments/pnckfv/trouble_mo ving_on/.

Reddit. "The Calm Before The Storm." Reddit, January 11, 2018. https:// web.archive.org/web/20180111150259/https://www.reddit.com/r/C BTS_Stream/.

Reneau, Annie. "A Former QAnon Believer Answers All Your Questions about How the Cult Really Works." Upworthy, January 26, 2021. http s://www.upworthy.com/former-qanon-believer-q-and-a.

Reyes, Antonio. "Strategies of Legitimization in Political Discourse: From Words to Actions." *Discourse & Society* 22, no. 6 (November 2011): 781–807. https://doi.org/10.1177/0957926511419927.

Romano, Aja. "YouTube's Most Popular User Amplified Anti-Semitic Rhetoric. Again." Vox, December 13, 2018. https://www.vox.com/20 18/12/13/18136253/pewdiepie-vs-tseries-links-to-white-supremacist -alt-right-redpill.

Roose, Kevin. "On Gab, an Extremist-Friendly Site, Pittsburgh Shooting Suspect Aired His Hatred in Full." *The New York Times*, October 28, 2018, sec. U.S. https://www.nytimes.com/2018/10/28/us/gab-robert -bowers-pittsburgh-synagogue-shootings.html.

———. "The Alt-Right Created a Parallel Internet. It's an Unholy Mess." *The New York Times*, December 11, 2017, sec. Technology. https://www .nytimes.com/2017/12/11/technology/alt-right-internet.html.

———. "The Making of a YouTube Radical." *The New York Times*, June 8, 2019. https://www.nytimes.com/interactive/2019/06/08/technolo gy/youtube-radical.html, https://www.nytimes.com/interactive/20 19/06/08/technology/youtube-radical.html.

Rose, E. M. *The Murder of William of Norwich: The Origins of the Blood Libel in Medieval Europe*. Oxford: Oxford University Press, 2015.

Royzman, Edward, Clark McCauley, and Paul Rozin. "From Plato to Put-nam: Four Ways to Think About Hate." In *The Psychology of Hate*, edited by Robert Sternberg, 3–35. Washington, D.C.: American Psycholog-ical Association, 2005.

Saldaña, Johnny. *The Coding Manual for Qualitative Researchers*. London, UK: Sage, 2013.

Sandifer, Elizabeth. *Neoreaction: A Basilisk*. Wooster, OH: Eruditorum Press, 2017.

Sardarizadeh, Shayan. "Parler 'free Speech' App Tops Charts in Wake of Trump Defeat." *BBC News*, November 9, 2020, sec. Technology. https://www.bbc.com/news/technology-54873800.

Sartre, Jean-Paul. *Anti-Semite and Jew*. Translated by George J Becker. New York: Schocken Books, 1948.

Scaptura, Maria N., and Kaitlin M. Boyle. "Masculinity Threat, 'Incel' Traits, and Violent Fantasies Among Heterosexual Men in the United States." *Feminist Criminology* 15, no. 3 (July 1, 2020): 278–98. https://doi.org/10.1177/1557085119896415.

Schieber, Jonathan. "Parler Jumps to No. 1 on App Store after Facebook and Twitter Ban Trump." *TechCrunch* (blog). Accessed September 30, 2021. https://social.techcrunch.com/2021/01/09/parler-jumps-to-no-1-on-app-store-after-facebook-and-twitter-bans/.

Schmitt, Carl. *Political Theology: Four Chapters on the Concept of Sovereignty*. Chicago: University of Chicago Press, 2005.

Schraderopolis2020. "I Used to Think QAnon Was Funny, Then It Became the Largest Cult in World History." Reddit Post. *R/QAnonCasualties*, April 25, 2021. www.reddit.com/r/QAnonCasualties/comments/myhnb6/i_used_to_think_qanon_was_funny_then_it_became/.

Schreckinger, Ben. "Amid Censorship Fears, Trump Campaign 'checking out' Alternative Social Network." POLITICO, May 28, 2019. https://politi.co/2KePraW.

Schwartz, Josh. "How One QAnon Believer Escaped The 'Grand Unified Theory Of All Conspiracy Theories.'" Accessed October 26, 2021. https://www.wbur.org/endlessthread/2020/10/02/qanon-casualties-conspiracy-theory.

Schwarzenegger, Christian, and Anna Wagner. "Can It Be Hate If It Is Fun? Discursive Ensembles of Hatred and Laughter in Extreme Right Satire on Facebook." *Studies in Communication | Media* 7, no. 4 (2018): 473–98. https://doi.org/10.5771/2192-4007-2018-4-473.

Sear, Richard F., Nicolás Velásquez, Rhys Leahy, Nicholas Johnson Restrepo, Sara El Oud, Nicholas Gabriel, Yonatan Lupu, and Neil F. Johnson. "Quantifying COVID-19 Content in the Online Health

Opinion War Using Machine Learning." *IEEE Access* 8 (2020): 91886–93. https://doi.org/10.1109/ACCESS.2020.2993967.

See, Rose. "From Crumbs to Conspiracy: Qanon as a Community of Hermeneutic Practice." Senior Thesis, Swarthmore College, 2019.

Shafak, Elif. "To Understand the Far Right, Look to Their Bookshelves." *The Guardian*, April 1, 2019. https://www.theguardian.com/commen tisfree/2019/apr/01/far-right-bookshelves-jordan-peterson-thilo-s arrazin.

Shand, Alexander. *The Foundations of Character*. The Foundations of Character, 2nd Ed. Oxford: Macmillan, 1920.

SillyWhabbit. "I Just Heard from My Q." Reddit Post. *R/ReQovery*, May 19, 2021. www.reddit.com/r/ReQovery/comments/nftkjv/i_just_hea rd_from_my_q/.

Silverstein, Jason. "Robert Bowers, Pittsburgh Shooting Suspect, Was Avid Poster of Anti-Semitic Content on Gab." CBS News, October 28, 2018. https://www.cbsnews.com/news/robert-bowers-gab-pittsbur gh-shooting-suspect-today-live-updates-2018-10-27/.

Silverstone, Roger. *Why Study the Media?* London, UK: Sage, 1999.

Sloterdijk, Peter. *Rage and Time: A Psychopolitical Investigation*. Columbia University Press, 2012.

Smith, Mark Caleb. "QAnon, Conspiracy Theories, and Evangelicals." Accessed September 25, 2020. https://myfaithradio.com/program_ podcast/qanon-conspiracy-theories-evangelicals-worldwide-move ment-prayer-repentance/.

Solomos, John, and Les Back. *Racism and Society*. London: Macmillan, 1996.

Solzhenitsyn, Aleksandr. *The Gulag Archipelago: An Experiment in Literary Investigation*. Vol. 1. London: Vintage, 2020.

Spalding, Elizabeth Edwards. "'We Must Put on the Armor of God': Harry Truman and the Cold War." In *Religion and the American Presidency*, 95–118. London: Springer, 2007.

Stanley-Becker, Isaac. "'We Are Q': A Deranged Conspiracy Cult Leaps from the Internet to the Crowd at Trump's 'MAGA' Tour." *Washington Post*, August 1, 2018. https://www.washingtonpost.com/news/morn

ing-mix/wp/2018/08/01/we-are-q-a-deranged-conspiracy-cult-lea
ps-from-the-internet-to-the-crowd-at-trumps-maga-tour/.

Steinbuch, Yaron. "Suspect in Deadly Attack on Muslim Family Had No
Known Ties to Hate Groups." *New York Post*, June 9, 2021. https://nyp
ost.com/2021/06/09/suspect-in-attack-on-muslim-family-had-no-
known-ties-to-hate-groups/.

Stevenson, Alexandra. "Facebook Admits It Was Used to Incite Violence
in Myanmar." *The New York Times*, November 6, 2018, sec. Technology. https://www.nytimes.com/2018/11/06/technology/myanmar-fa
cebook.html.

Steyerl, Hito. "A Sea of Data: Apophenia and Pattern (Mis-)Recognition."
E-Flux, no. 72 (April 2016). https://www.e-flux.com/journal/72/6048
0/a-sea-of-data-apophenia-and-pattern-mis-recognition/.

Stone, Natalie. "YouTuber PewDiePie Calls Lilly Singh a 'Crybaby' After She Speaks Out About Wage Inequality." *People*, December 10,
2018. https://people.com/tv/youtube-pewdiepie-calls-lilly-singh-cr
ybaby-wage-gap/.

Stroop, Chrissy. "Behind a Recent Stunt in Idaho Lies a Dangerous
Theocratic Movement." Religion Dispatches, June 29, 2020. https://r
eligiondispatches.org/behind-a-recent-stunt-in-idaho-lies-a-dang
erous-theocratic-movement/.

sumterwinner. "Boss and Job." Reddit Post. *R/QAnonCasualties*, October
19, 2021. www.reddit.com/r/QAnonCasualties/comments/qbcimz/b
oss_and_job/.

Tavernise, Sabrina. "'Trump Just Used Us and Our Fear': One Woman's
Journey Out of QAnon." *The New York Times*, January 29, 2021,
sec. U.S. https://www.nytimes.com/2021/01/29/us/leaving-qanon-c
onspiracy.html.

Theweleit, Klaus. *Male Fantasies: Women, Floods, Bodies, History*. Vol. 1.
Cambridge: Polity Press, 1987.

Thiel, David, Renée DiResta, Shelby Grossman, and Elena Cryst. "Contours and Controversies of Parler." Stanford, CA: Stanford Internet
Observatory, January 2021.

Thurston, Nick. "Back to Front Truths." In *Post-Digital Cultures of the Far Right*, edited by Maik Fielitz and Nick Thurston, 193–204. transcript Verlag, 2018.

Timberg, Craig, and Isaac Stanley-Becker. "QAnon Learns to Survive — and Even Thrive — after Silicon Valley's Crackdown." *Washington Post*, October 29, 2020. https://www.washingtonpost.com/technology/20 20/10/28/qanon-crackdown-election/.

Torba, Andrew. *An Update On Gab*, 2019. https://www.youtube.com/watc h?v=eUTHRTfgOsk&feature=youtu.be&app=desktop.

———. "Building Technology To Power A Parallel Christian Society." *Gab News* (blog), September 27, 2021. https://news.gab.com/2021/09/27/ building-technology-to-power-a-parallel-christian-society/.

———. "Happy 3rd Birthday, Gab.Com." *Gab News* (blog), August 15, 2019. https://news.gab.com/2019/08/15/happy-3rd-birthday-gab-com/.

———. "Our Daughter Turns 2 Today." Gab Social, July 26, 2021. https:// gab.com/a/posts/106643483539713788.

Truthwins24_7. "A Chink in the Q Armour...." Reddit Post. R/ *QAnonCasualties*, October 17, 2021. www.reddit.com/r/QAnonC asualties/comments/qa7rzw/a_chink_in_the_q_armour/.

Tso, Matt, and Catrin Owen. "Video Captures Act of Bravery as Police Arrest Christchurch Shooting Suspect." Stuff, March 16, 2019. https://www.stuff.co.nz/national/crime/111328483/video-capt ures-moment-police-arrested-shooting-suspected.

Tuters, Marc, Emilija Jokubauskaitė, and Daniel Bach. "Post-Truth Protest: How 4chan Cooked up the Pizzagate Bullshit." *M/C Journal* 21, no. 3 (2018).

Twitter. "Progress on Addressing Online Abuse," November 15, 2016. htt ps://blog.twitter.com/en_us/a/2016/progress-on-addressing-onlin e-abuse.html.

Uscinski, Joseph E., Casey Klofstad, and Matthew D. Atkinson. "What Drives Conspiratorial Beliefs? The Role of Informational Cues and Predispositions." *Political Research Quarterly* 69, no. 1 (2016): 57–71.

Vincent, James. "Former Facebook Exec Says Social Media Is Ripping Apart Society." *The Verge*, December 11, 2017. https://www.theverge.

com/2017/12/11/16761016/former-facebook-exec-ripping-apart-soci
ety.

Vosoughi, Soroush, Deb Roy, and Sinan Aral. "The Spread of True and False News Online." *Science* 359, no. 6380 (March 9, 2018): 1146–51. https://doi.org/10.1126/science.aap9559.

Wachowski, Lana, and Lilly Wachowski. *The Matrix*, 1998. https://www.dailyscript.com/scripts/the_matrix.pdf.

Wallace, Anthony F. C. "Mazeway Resynthesis: A Biocultural Theory of Religious Inspiration*." *Transactions of the New York Academy of Sciences* 18, no. 7 Series II (1956): 626–38. https://doi.org/10.1111/j.2164-0947.1956.tb00491.x.

Wamsley, Laura. "On Far-Right Websites, Plans To Storm Capitol Were Made In Plain Sight." NPR.org, January 7, 2021. https://www.npr.org/sections/insurrection-at-the-capitol/2021/01/07/954671745/on-far-right-websites-plans-to-storm-capitol-were-made-in-plain-sight.

Wendling, Mike. *Alt-Right: From 4chan to the White House*. London: Pluto Press, 2018.

Wiant, Fredel M. "Exploiting Factional Discourse: Wedge Issues in Contemporary American Political Campaigns." *Southern Journal of Communication* 67, no. 3 (2002): 276–89.

Williams, Matthew L., Pete Burnap, Amir Javed, Han Liu, and Sefa Ozalp. "Hate in the Machine: Anti-Black and Anti-Muslim Social Media Posts as Predictors of Offline Racially and Religiously Aggravated Crime." *The British Journal of Criminology* 60, no. 1 (January 1, 2020): 93–117. https://doi.org/10.1093/bjc/azz049.

Wilson, Andrew. "#whitegenocide, the Alt-Right and Conspiracy Theory: How Secrecy and Suspicion Contributed to the Mainstreaming of Hate." *Secrecy and Society* 1, no. 2 (2018): 49.

Wilson, Andrew Fergus. "Conspiracy Theories, Millennialism, and the Nation: Understanding the Collective Voice in Improvisational Millennialism." University of Derby, 2020. http://hdl.handle.net/10545/625070.

Wilson, Jason. "Hiding in Plain Sight: How the 'alt-Right' Is Weaponizing Irony to Spread Fascism." *The Guardian*, May 23, 2017. https://ww

w.theguardian.com/technology/2017/may/23/alt-right-online-hum
or-as-a-weapon-facism.

Wodak, Ruth. *The Politics of Fear: What Right-Wing Populist Discourses Mean*.
London: Sage, 2015.

———. "Vom Rand in die Mitte—„Schamlose Normalisierung"." *Politi-sche Vierteljahresschrift* 59, no. 2 (June 1, 2018): 323–35. https://doi.org
/10.1007/s11615-018-0079-7.

Wood, Graeme. "His Kampf." *The Atlantic*, June 2017. https://www.theatl
antic.com/magazine/archive/2017/06/his-kampf/524505/.

Woolley, Samuel, Roya Pakzad, and Nicholas Monaco. "Incubating Hate:
Islamophobia and Gab." Washington, D.C.: German Marshall Fund &
Institute for the Future, June 21, 2019. http://www.gmfus.org/sites
/default/files/publications/pdf/Incubating%20Hate%20-%20Islamo
phobia%20and%20Gab.pdf.

Yancy, George. *What White Looks like: African-American Philosophers on the
Whiteness Question*. Routledge, 2004.

Zadrozny, Brandy, and Ben Collins. "Who Is behind the Qanon Con-spiracy? We've Traced It to Three People." NBC News, August 15,
2018. https://www.nbcnews.com/tech/tech-news/how-three-consp
iracy-theorists-took-q-sparked-qanon-n900531.

Zannettou, Savvas, Barry Bradlyn, Emiliano De Cristofaro, Haewoon
Kwak, Michael Sirivianos, Gianluca Stringhini, and Jeremy Black-burn. "What Is Gab? A Bastion of Free Speech or an Alt-Right Echo
Chamber?" *Companion of the The Web Conference 2018*, 2018, 1007–14. h
ttps://doi.org/10.1145/3184558.3191531.

Zannettou, Savvas, Joel Finkelstein, Barry Bradlyn, and Jeremy Black-burn. "A Quantitative Approach to Understanding Online Anti-semitism." *ArXiv:1809.01644 [Cs]*, November 24, 2019. http://arxiv.o
rg/abs/1809.01644.

Zezima, Katie, and Wesley Lowery. "Suspected Synagogue Shooter
Appears to Have Railed against Jews, Refugees Online." *Washington
Post*, October 28, 2018. https://www.washingtonpost.com/national/
suspected-synagogue-shooter-appears-to-have-railed-against-jew
s-refugees-online/2018/10/27/e99dd282-da18-11e8-a10f-b51546b107
56_story.html.

Zhang, Ziqi, and Lei Luo. "Hate Speech Detection: A Solved Problem? The Challenging Case of Long Tail on Twitter." *Semantic Web* 10, no. 5 (January 1, 2019): 925–45. https://doi.org/10.3233/SW-180338.

Zhou, Yuchen, Mark Dredze, David A Broniatowski, and William D Adler. "Elites and Foreign Actors among the Alt-Right: The Gab Social Media Platform." *First Monday* 24, no. 9 (2019).

Zuckerberg, Donna. "How the Alt-Right Is Weaponizing the Classics." Medium, October 15, 2018. https://medium.com/s/story/how-the-alt-right-is-weaponizing-the-classics-d4c1c8dfcb73.

Zuckerman, Ethan. "QAnon and the Emergence of the Unreal." *Journal of Design and Science*, no. 6 (July 15, 2019). https://doi.org/10.21428/7808da6b.6b8a82b9.

Bielefeld University Press

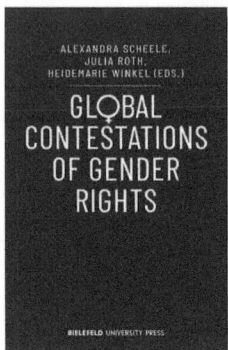

Alexandra Scheele, Julia Roth, Heidemarie Winkel (eds.)
Global Contestations of Gender Rights

2022, 354 p., pb., col. ill.
40,00 € (DE), 978-3-8376-6069-2
E-Book: available as free open access publication
PDF: ISBN 978-3-8394-6069-6

Silke Schwandt (ed.)
Digital Methods in the Humanities
Challenges, Ideas, Perspectives

2020, 312 p., pb., col. ill.
38,00 € (DE), 978-3-8376-5419-6
E-Book: available as free open access publication
PDF: ISBN 978-3-8394-5419-0

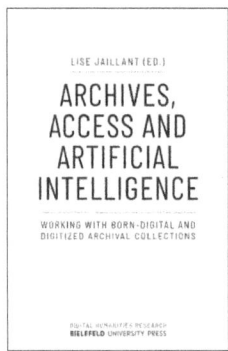

Lise Jaillant (ed.)
Archives, Access and Artificial Intelligence
Working with Born-Digital
and Digitized Archival Collections

2022, 224 p., pb., col. ill.
45,00 € (DE), 978-3-8376-5584-1
E-Book: available as free open access publication
PDF: ISBN 978-3-8394-5584-5

**All print, e-book and open access versions of the titles in our list
are available in the online shop www.bielefeld-university-press.de**

Bielefeld University Press

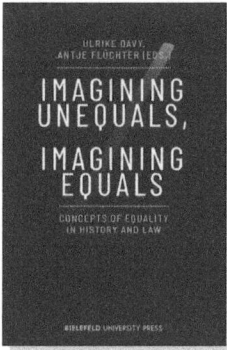

Ulrike Davy, Antje Flüchter (eds.)
Imagining Unequals, Imagining Equals
Concepts of Equality in History and Law

2022, 258 p., pb., col. ill.
35,00 € (DE), 978-3-8376-5887-3
E-Book: available as free open access publication
PDF: ISBN 978-3-8394-5887-7

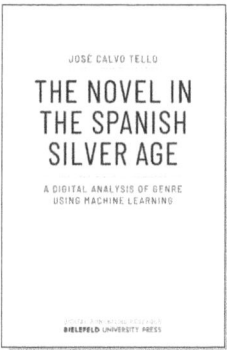

José Calvo Tello
The Novel in the Spanish Silver Age
A Digital Analysis of Genre Using Machine Learning

2021, 470 p., pb., col. ill.
48,00 € (DE), 978-3-8376-5925-2
E-Book: available as free open access publication
PDF: ISBN 978-3-8394-5925-6

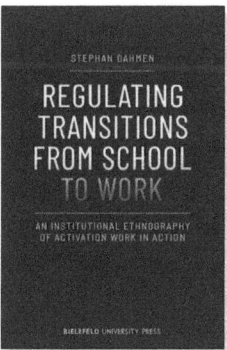

Stephan Dahmen
Regulating Transitions from School to Work
An Institutional Ethnography
of Activation Work in Action

2021, 312 p., pb., ill.
36,00 € (DE), 978-3-8376-5706-7
E-Book: available as free open access publication
PDF: ISBN 978-3-8394-5706-1

**All print, e-book and open access versions of the titles in our list
are available in the online shop www.bielefeld-university-press.de**

GPSR Authorized Representative: Easy Access System Europe, Mustamäe tee
50, 10621 Tallinn, Estonia, gpsr.requests@easproject.com

www.ingramcontent.com/pod-product-compliance
Lightning Source LLC
Chambersburg PA
CBHW070109030426
42335CB00016B/2070